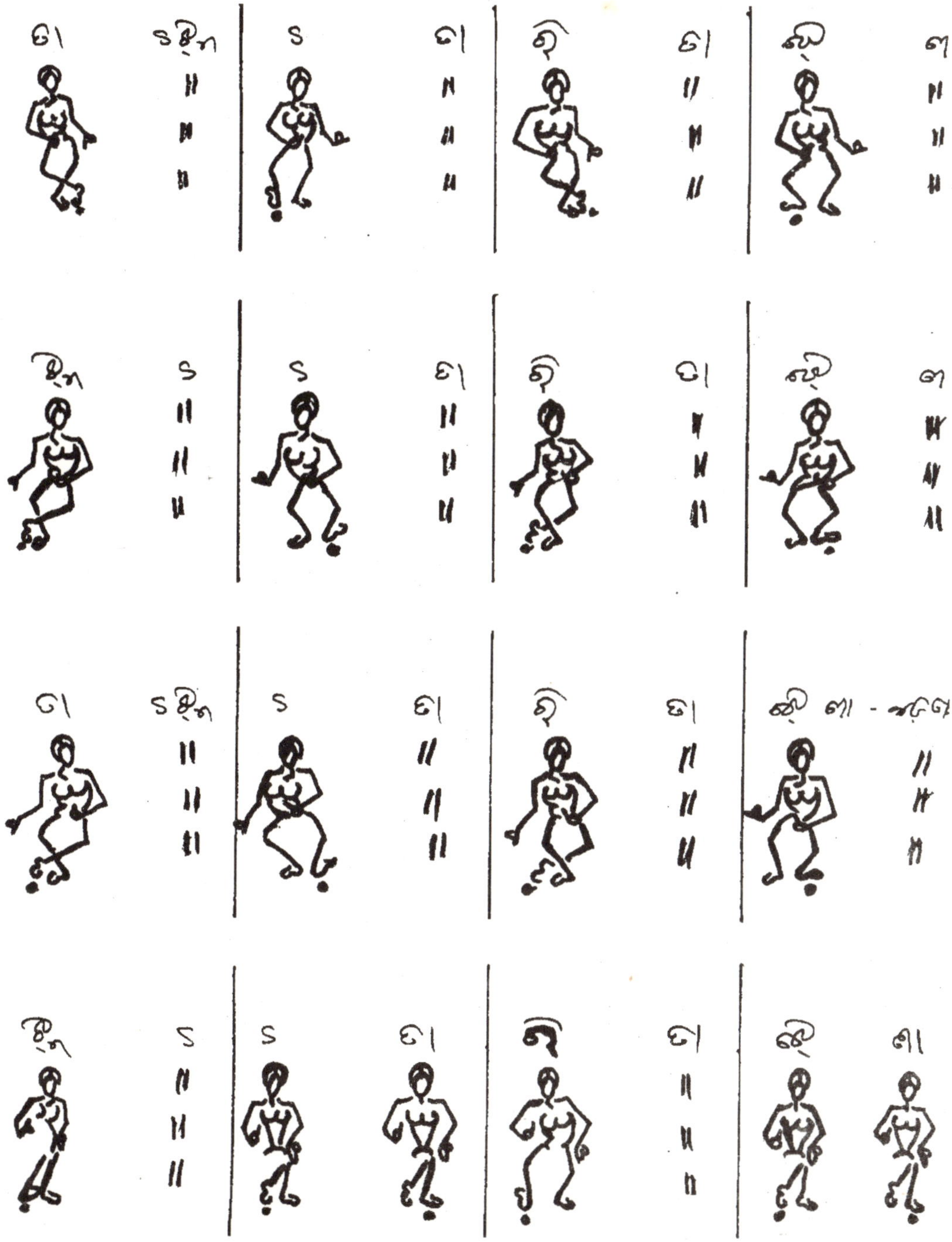

The Making of a Guru

KELUCHARAN MOHAPATRA
His Life and Times

The Making of a Guru

KELUCHARAN MOHAPATRA
His Life and Times

ILEANA CITARISTI

MANOHAR
2015

First published 2001
Reprinted 2005, 2015

ISBN 978-81-7304-369-7

Published by

Ajay Kumar Jain *for*
Manohar Publishers & Distributors
4753/23 Ansari Road, Daryaganj
New Delhi 110 002

Printed at

Salasar Imaging Systems
Delhi 110 035

TO

MY PARENTS

ROSA

AND

SEVERINO

CONTENTS

ILLUSTRATIONS

PREFACE

THIS BOOK is a homage to the creative genius of Guru Kelucharan Mohapatra. As one of the hundreds whose life has been touched and transformed by this great guru, I wish to express my gratitude through this humble and certainly inadequate effort.

The story of his artistic experience touches all the salient aspects of the cultural life of Orissa in the last 60 years, and is the story of the growth of Odissi and its recognition as a classical dance form.

From the traditional expertize of the *chitrakaras*, through the entertaining art forms of the Gotipua and Jatra parties, the *bhakti* oriented Ras Leela performances and the innovative attempts of the Annapurna Theatre Groups, Kelucharan's artistic journey is a continuous and dedicated search for excellence. In the course of the journey he has learnt from his rich and varied experience and grown in stature.

His attitude towards the world, his dance, his style of teaching and his playing on the pakhawaj all share a quality of 'vivid reality', something which has been acquired not through formal learning but through a continuous interaction with life.

For him, building a brick wall, constructing a roof or composing a delicate dance piece for Jayadeva's lyrics are all actions permeated by the same degree of intensity and artistry. His life represents an unending creative process unfolding itself in the creativity of nature.

ILEANA CITARISTI

ACKNOWLEDGEMENTS

IN THE ABSENCE of any written documentation, especially of the events in the first 40 years of Kelucharan's life, I had to collect most of the data from the oral testimony of people who were part of the history of the Odissi dance in its making. The authenticating of the data has been cross-checked by interviewing a number of individuals who had been part of that cultural scene; despite this there are bound to be omissions and mistakes for which I apologize. I also apologize for the quality of some of the photographs which are included for their archival value.

Although most of the information was given to me by Guruji himself, tnere were many others who spared their valuable time and shared their memories of that period with me. I wish to thank all of them and let them know how much I enjoyed meeting them.

In particular I wish to thank Itishree Panda and Jatindra Nayak for making my English more intelligible, and Kumkum Lal for her valuable suggestions regarding the content. Last but not least I wish to thank the then Secretary of Culture, Mr. B.P. Singh, for granting a Senior Fellowship of the Human Resource Development Ministry which enabled me to undertake this valuable project.

I am grateful to Kalamani Rabindra Nath Sahu (NA), Bhubaneswar for supplying the decorative motifs appearing in this book.

ILEANA CITARISTI

CHILDHOOD

IT HAS NOT been possible to find out the exact date of Kelucharan's birth. Until recently, we used to celebrate his birthday on 1 August, assuming the year of his birth to be 1926. But, four or five years ago his birthday was shifted to the lunar month of *Paus* (December-January) and judging by his life story it seems to me that he must have been born around the year 1924. The only written document which could have helped in this matter, his palm leaf horoscope, had been given away to an astrologer when Kelucharan was ill and was never returned. The date which the astrologer wrote down in English, most probably in a hurry, jealously preserved by Kelucharan's wife among the sacred relics of the house, does not help either; it mentions the year of his birth as 1934, which would leave the chronological sequence of the events in his life in total disorder.

On the other hand, the place of his birth is not only certain but has also remained more or less the same as it must have been 70 years ago! Surrounded by a rich grove of coconut palms, mango and jack-fruit trees, the village of Raghurajpur is encircled on three sides by the river Bhargavi and precariously connected with the main road which leads to Puri through a narrow embankment lane which becomes totally inaccessible during the rainy season. The village, hidden by the grove, appears suddenly after a left turn of the road, and consists of a row of six small temples—like a coral string in the middle—flanked on both sides by two lines of houses with high steps and small verandas in front.

The first of these temples, a tiny structure concealed among the roots of a huge banyan tree, is the abode of goddess Bhuasuni, to whom the village women offer their children for protection. Little Kelu was also offered by his mother to the goddess when he was ill with chickenpox at the age of four. She literally left him at her feet telling the goddess that from now on the child was her son and she could do what she wanted with him. A few days later, a *kalisi*[1] came to their house and touched the boy's eyes chanting some sacred mantra: slowly the little child started to recover. It seems that the mother at this point wanted to perform a puja for getting her son back but the child refused and the puja was never performed.

The name 'Kelu' was given to him when he was about three years old; originally he had been called Madana Mohana, an appellative of Lord Krishna. It so happened that a couple of years after his birth, his sister Champa, a year older than him, passed away; and when his younger brother too, died a few months after birth, his parents started to worry. They felt that the combination of the child's *rasi* and his illustrious name was perhaps too potent and was turning out to be dangerous for his siblings; so a new name had to be found which would counteract the influence of his strong constellation. The name 'Kela'—denoting low-caste man who wanders from village to village with a basket of snakes begging for his livelihood—was suggested by his maternal grandmother Nilamani. In order to soften its impact, the appellative 'Baba' was prefixed to it. Among the much respected names of his brothers and sisters such as Ganesh, Ekadasi, Champa, Bhagawan, Nisha and Bansidhar, 'Baba Kela' was the little 'outcaste'.

Kelucharan's house was on the side of the Gopinath Mandir, the fourth one in the row. A few houses ahead was the *chatasali*, a sort of veranda where the village children were sent to learn to read and write. When Kelucharan joined the school he was five years old and during the three years of his irregular attendance all that he managed to learn was the Oriya alphabet and numbers up to ten. The teacher was not too popular among the students; Kelucharan remembers him drawing *pata chitra* sitting all the while, with a long stick lying by his side. Once in a while he would suddenly raise his eyes and hit a student taking him by surprise. In retaliation the naughtiest among the pupils, Gopinath, Kelucharan and Shyamo, would never miss a chance of

[1] *Kalisi* is a mediator between the goddess and the villagers; when possessed by her spirit he would get into a trance which would enable him to operate on her behalf.

Kelucharan's younger brother, Bansidhar, painting papier mâché toys in his house at Raghurajpur.

troubling the teacher. Once they spread thorns over his seat and then went into hiding for three days on top of a *tala* tree (a variety of palm tree) to escape his wrath.

School had never been Kelucharan's favourite place; too many things were happening in that small village which were much more interesting to learn than the knowledge the surly teacher had to impart. Legend has it that Lord Rama and his wife Sita, while in exile in the forest, took shelter in the nearby Bhrugunrusingha Ashram. And in return for the hospitality provided by the rishis, they allowed the village as well as the surrounding area to be named after them, that is Janakadeipur. It is believed that even Chaitanya Mahaprabhu visited the village on his way to Puri and the river Danda Bhanga derived its name from the stick thrown away by him at this point of his journey.

Once a year, during the Vasanta Utsava (the spring festival), starting with the full moon in the month of March and continuing for ten days, a grand assemblage of the idols of Radha-Krishna and Sita-Rama from all the villages of Janakadeipur area took place in the big field bordering the village. While the idols would just remain installed on their palanquins for eight days, it was the last two days of the festival that saw a real frenzy of music, rhythm and dance. A wide variety of all performing art traditions of the area such as Sankirtana, Naga dance, Stick play, Bear dance, Krishna Leela and Jatra were offered in a joyous and competitive spirit before the idols.

During all the major festivals of the year, Durga Puja, Kartika Puja, Laxmi Puja, Saraswati Puja, Dola Jatra, etc., (it is said that in Puri thirteen such festivals are celebrated during the 12 months), Jatra parties from nearby villages would come to Raghurajpur and perform all night in front of the Gopinath Mandir, just a few yards from Kelucharan's house. Dance, drama, music, rhythm all combined to recreate imaginative stories of the past and present. Raghurajpur itself had its own Jatra party and boys just a few years older than Kelucharan were already acting in it. Jagannath Mohapatra, who was the first artist to receive a National Award for *pata* painting, used to play the role of the hero and Maguni Das, who has still kept alive the tradition of the *gotipua* dance in the village, played the heroine. Kelucharan's paternal uncle, Ananda, already a famous dholak player, used to accompany the local Jatra

Jatra in progress at Raghurajpur.

Jagannath Mohapatra receives the Shilpi Shramdana award from Biju Patnaik during the Vasanta Utsava celebration in Raghurajpur, April 1996. To the right is Kelucharan Mohapatra.

party wherever they performed. Since he was a little boy, Kelu had to be content only with a minor role in a group dance performed by small children holding sticks in their hands. Despite that it was exciting for him to be near his heroes, watch their powerful acting, with gorgeous make-ups and extravagant costumes, amplified by the flickering lights of the torches playing on their faces.

Every evening, a local group of percussionists and singers would assemble in front of Sri Gouranga Mandir, the sixth temple in the row, and from there a procession would wend its way around the entire village singing and chanting Sanskrit *slokas* to the accompaniment of percussion instruments such as the mridanga, jhanja and manjira. A Sankirtana group consists of a minimum of twelve members, out of which ten constitute the *palia* or chorus who play the percussions and the other two are singers who recite and sing the *slokas*. This practice goes back to Chaitanya and his descendants, under whose care the Gouranga Mandir has been placed, and to date their permission is sought before the ceremony begins. If the recitation of Sanskrit *slokas* and singing of Vaishnava songs are an important component of a Sankirtana performance, the powerful and intricate rhythmic interludes are equally

A group of Sankirtana players at Raghurajpur.

so. The mridanga or khol is the basic percussion instrument used in a Sankirtana ensemble; it is a double-faced horizontal drum made out of clay and is considered to be the precursor of the wooden ones, the dholak, mardal and tabla.[2] The *bani* or *bols* used in the playing of mridanga are peculiar to this instrument and are a mixture of words and cadenced syllables grouped in 18 different basic combinations.

Kelucharan's father, Chintamani Mohapatra, besides being a *pata chitra* painter by caste was also an excellent khol player. Little Kelu would never miss a chance to sit beside his father or his uncle Ananda, and copy the movements of their hands on whatever object he could lay his hands on, be it a colour box or his buttocks.

[2] According to a legend the *mrutu-anga* (clay body) of the first drum was so fragile that Shiva created a similar one in wood and found that it was 'sounding well' ('*pakkha-awaj*' from which the name pakhawaj is said to have derived). The Muslims broke it into two and found that this shape was also 'sounding well'('*tabi balla*' which led to the name 'tabla').

But what really excited him was the sound coming from a little house next to the *chatasali*. Every morning, on his way to the school Kelucharan could never resist peering inside it. He would stand there for hours, half hidden by the veranda pillar, without having the courage either to enter or to walk away from this house. When Guru Balabhadra Sahu realized that the child was coming every morning to watch him teach, he invited little Kelucharan inside one day and asked him to repeat what he had seen. The little child, hardly five years old, began on his first lessons in dance thus.

Balabhadra Sahu was not a native of Raghurajpur; he had come here with his family from another village. Although he had been there for a long time, he was still ostracized by the villagers. While the *akhada* on the other side of the village, where Mohan Maharana and Agadhu Maharana taught dancing, had a number of students and were given opportunities to perform, this one, which Kelucharan joined, had only one student and almost no opportunities to perform anywhere. The guru was a *gudia* (confectioner) by caste and would leave in the morning with a basket full of *ukhuda*, *khoja*, *peda* and *jilebi*[3] on his head and come back in the evening after having purchased rice and vegetables with the day's earning. Kelucharan remembers him as an extremely gentle person, dedicated and hard-working. He excelled in the art of *abhinaya*, especially in the portrayal of female roles; he was adept not only in singing and the *gotipua* dance but also in playing the mardala and violin.

Every morning for about three years Kelucharan went to the *akhada* to learn from Balabhadra Sahu, and in his absence he would be under the care of Panua, the only other student at the *akhada*. Kelucharan's father would visit the nearby Kapoteswara Temple early morning for his daily rituals; the walk to the temple, the bath, the puja and trudging back home—all these activities took about two hours. This was the time Kelucharan had at his disposal for attending the classes at the *akhada* without his father's knowledge.

Although it is not exactly known when this art of the *gotipua* or boys dancing in female attire came into being, there is evidence that during the early Vaishnava period, soon after Chaitanya's time, this dance form was used to promote the Vaishnava cult and philosophy, emphasizing

[3] Different type of sweets made out of milk, sweetened rice and sugar syrup.

Gotipua *dance during Ganesh Puja celebration in a* matha *at Puri.*

[4] Chandan Jatra starts three days after the *amavasya* in the month of *Baisakha* (April-May) and lasts for 21 days. During this period in the evening, the *murti* of Jagannath and his consort are taken out for a ride on a white boat in the Narendra Tank. On a second boat, red in colour, five images of Mahadeva and one of Rama-Krishna are placed; while on the first boat, the *devadasi* used to dance, on the second, the dance was performed by the *sahi pilla*. The Jhoolan Jatra starts seven days before the full moon of the month of *Shravan* (July-August) and lasts until the night of the full moon. During the week, in the evening, after dinner, the *murti* of Radha-Krishna, placed on a swing in the *mukti mandapa* built inside the temple compound, is entertained by the dance of the *sahi pilla*.

the *sakhi bhava* or offering oneself to Krishna as a female attendant. During the Afghan and Muslim invasions in the sixteenth and seventeenth centuries respectively, political and religious life in Orissa was in turmoil and many of the rituals associated with the temple of Lord Jagannath in Puri were in danger of being discontinued. Among these, was the dances of the *maharis* or female servants of God, especially those performed during the rituals for the Lord outside the premises. In all probability it must have been at this point of time that boys were encouraged and trained by the temple servants to perform and sing during festivals like the Jhoolan Jatra and Chandan Jatra[4] when the idol of Madana Mohana, representative of Lord Jagannath, was brought outside the sanctum sanctorum of the temple.

While the prerogative to dance inside the temple proper continued to remain with the *maharis*, the *sahi pilla*, as these boys were called, performed as their substitutes outside the temple. With the establishment of *akhadas* or gymnasiums in each street of Puri, in order to develop a physical culture to protect the temple and the town from invaders, the practice of training boys in dance accompanied with the teaching of different martial art skills. The boys trained in the *akhada*, known as *akhada pilla*, although not connected with the rituals of Lord Jagannath, propagated the Vaishnava cult since the songs portrayed in their dance were mostly based on the Radha-Krishna theme. In time they came to be employed and sometimes patronized by zamindars all over coastal Orissa and were even called in as *gotipua dala* (professional groups) to entertain guests at public functions.

While this helped the boys to earn their livelihood and at the same time to spread the Vaishnava cult, the art form got corrupted by external influences. By the beginning of the twentieth century, it came to be looked upon by many as cheap and vulgar. Although there must have been a conspicuous tendency to 'play to the gallery' during the performances, with a view to entertaining their hosts and getting easy remuneration, it is also a fact that, after the decline of the *devadasi* cult, the *akhada* was the only centre of 'formal' training in dance in Orissa during the first half of the twentieth century. The particular way of rendering the songs and the combinations of rhythmic *bols* which were played on the mardal as accompaniment to the dance were known as Odissi and this was the name by which the dance came to be known later on. The training imparted included both the elements of *nritta* or rhythmic dance and *nritya* or interpretative dance although these had not yet been classified as distinct items.

The basic poses of *chowka* or symmetrical position of bent knees and *tribhanga* or triple flexions of the body were taught along with the uses of hand gestures called *parija* and their possible variations or *bohula*. The *gotipua* master may not have used the shastric terminology while teaching but he certainly developed his own system of mnemonic devices which could be understood by his young students (the average age of a *gotipua* dancer was between five and twelve years). For example, the *pataka* gesture (open hand

Kelucharan demonstrating the chowka *(above) and* tribhanga *(below) poses in Odissi style.*

with stretched fingers) would be taught as '*eka chappura maribi*' (I will give you a slap); the *kartari* (index and medium finger opened as a pair of scissors) as '*nakka kattidebi*' (I will cut your nose); the *kapittha* (index finger bent over the stretched thumb) as '*kana moridebi*' (I will twist your ear) and *ardhachandra* (thumb of the *pataka* hand stretched out) as '*galare dhaka dei bahara karidebi*' (Holding you by your throat I will throw you out).

During the three years of his training at the *akhada* Kelucharan had learnt besides some basic rhythmic combinations and footwork, the *abhinaya* for three Oriya songs: '*Leela nidhi he, lajjie mu galiti sari*' (oh best among all the pranksters, my shame has grown beyond all limits); '*Ajamu dekhili Shyamaku go*' (today I saw the dark god) and '*Kere sundara nabina natua*' (how beautiful is that young dancer). In the evenings, often he would either be watching rehearsals at the other *akhada* or sitting alongside his father at the *kirtan*. If little Kelucharan succeeded in learning from Balabhadra Sahu for full three years and in keeping it a secret from his father, a good part of the credit must go to his mother. Siri Nani, as she was affectionately called by everybody in the village, was in a way very different from her husband. While he was reserved and introverted, she was very friendly and always ready to lend a helping hand to anyone in need. She was a small and frail figure with the typical round face and vivacious eyes of an Oriya woman, endowed with an extraordinary physical strength and capacity for endurance. Kelucharan inherited many of his mother's qualities, not only physically but above all from her strong personality.

She was extremely fond of music and theatre and would not miss an opportunity to assist at an all-night Jatra performance even if that meant walking a few miles from her village. It was she who first aroused Kelucharan's interest in the many dance poses carved on the outer walls of the Konark Temple; she along with a few friends had gone all the way to Konark by foot, covering the distance of about 70 km each way, to take a dip in the river Chandrabhaga. Her descriptions of those beautiful sculptures were so vivid that the little child—about six years old then—by closing his eyes, was virtually able to visualize them.

She hailed from the same village and was of the same caste as her husband. In a *chitrakara* family a woman does most of the physical work before the *pati* or canvas on which

Kelucharan with his mother Siri Nani in the early 1980s.

the painting is done is prepared. The cutting of *hensa*,[5] drying and spreading it as a base over which pieces of coarse rags soaked in water and glue are placed till they become dry, then plastering and cutting it to the required size are activities done by the women of the house. Later this base is sprinkled with water and is polished for an entire day with a special stone or *chikana pathara* until it acquires a pale yellow shade and is ready for the application of the first coat of paint.

Although the actual painting is usually done by the men in the family, women are often involved in the preparation of the natural colours which are used as a base for the *chitra*. The red (*pihuli*) and yellow (*haritala*) colours are obtained by grinding mineral stones into a powder which is then mixed with a little water and stored in the shape of small balls. At the time of painting a special juice obtained from the *kaitha* tree is mixed with water. The white colour is derived from white conches which have to be ground until they are reduced to granules and then boiled for a long time, until a thick layer of foam is formed. The foam is later skimmed and dried and used as a colour. The black colour is made out of the soot formed on a brass surface placed on top of a flame.

Kelucharan remembers his mother being always busy

[5] A type of reed which grows in the marshes and is used in the preparation of mats to sleep during winter.

with one or the other of these chores; going around with buckets of glue on her head or returning from the river carrying tall pots (amphorae) brimming with water.

He would often sit with her listening to the fascinating stories she would narrate while painting. These vivid and colourful stories would take shape in front of his eyes: the ten incarnations of Vishnu; the story of love between Usha, the beautiful daughter of Banasur and Aniruddha, the grandson of Lord Krishna; and the *Dasa Poi* tale, from the story written by the court poet, Yuga Vanja. Lord Jagannath along with Lord Krishna in amorous dalliance with Radha were the most painted figures. The reality of these characters, the stories attributed to them—recreated on the canvas, enacted on the stage, sung during the Sankirtan or retold by the women of the village—were so intermingled with one another that the dividing line between fact and fantasy became blurred. These different artistic expressions were endless attempts to give shape to the unfathomable; there was a continuity which ran through them and it was this continuity which offered a cohesive meaning to what would otherwise have been a meaningless existence.

Kelucharan spent the formative years of his childhood

A sakhi *applying* alata *on Radha's feet in a* pata chitra *painting.*

in this intense atmosphere saturated with rich images, colours and sounds, not confining his desire for learning to a few symbols on a blackboard, but absorbing whatever life around him had to offer. This is something he would continue to do all his life.

Balabhadra Sahu must have sensed the exceptional ability of his pupil to absorb, observe and recreate whatever stimulus was given to him; three years of training were over and that year he planned to have his young pupil dance during the forthcoming Durga Puja festivities when various performances would be held in front of the Durga Bhuja Temple, the third one in the row of temples in the village. Up until then Kelucharan's mother had kept the dance training a secret from his father; she had even managed to conceal the fact that Kelu had pierced his nose and ears in order to wear the typical ornaments of the *gotipua* dancer (*noli*, a ring shaped ornament for the nose and *phansiya* a similar one for the ears). But performing in public would most certainly require the permission of the father; she could not take this responsibility solely upon herself.

Chintamani was shocked on hearing that Kelu had been learning at the *gotipua akhada* all these years. A reserved man, he never involved himself in the affairs of others. He was a man of strong conviction, deeply religious and totally dedicated to his art and to his work.

His reaction to Balabhadra Sahu's request was a sharp 'no'.

'Would you like to dance around moving your hips, making faces with your tongue stretched out, winking at the zamindari to receive garlands of flowers or to get bank-notes pinned on your chest? This will not do!' he told little Kelu who was stunned by his father's harsh criticism. He had never imagined that his father held such a poor opinion of this dance; from that day onward he was forbidden to meet his guru. It was only at this point that he learnt that his guru was from another village and the fact that there was much opposition to him from the villagers; there was no way he could have approached him again. After this incident the guru did not remain in Raghurajpur for long; when Kelucharan returned to the village after a few years of absence he searched in vain for him. Nobody could tell him where he had gone; he had left embittered by what had happened.

Chintamani's reaction to Balabhadra's request may have

been dictated by more than one reason and may have been in good part a purely subjective one, but it is a fact that by the first decade of the twentieth century the *gotipua* dance form had been corrupted considerably by the incorporation of exaggerated mannerisms and cheap showmanship. These degenerative elements notwithstanding, it has to be acknowledged that without this crucial transitional stage the dance style which later came to be known as Odissi would probably not have come into existence. Whatever had remained of the original technique of the dance performed inside temples by the *maharis* was by now known only to a few among them since most of the members of this community by the beginning of this century had to resort to other sources of livelihood. Out of these two kinds of dances—one created in extreme seclusion by the 'servants of God' and the other, which had become an entirely commercial form of entertainment by the *gotipua* dancer—emerged a dance style that retained the best elements of the two. And by striking the right balance succeeded in becoming a classical dance form.

In spite of his strong opposition to his son training to become a *gotipua* dancer, Chintamani did not impose his own profession on Kelucharan; there were enough *chitrakaras* in the village who were impoverished by debts as they had lost their sources of livelihood. Most of them had to look for other means of livelihood to survive; some became wage-earners in betel leaf plantations, others became masons, agricultural labourers or actors in Jatra parties. By the beginning of this century, what was once a flourishing profession had been spoiled by unscrupulous middle men who took advantage of the ignorance and illiteracy of the craftspersons and managed to push them to the brink of ruin.

The *chitrakaras* of Raghurajpur, Danda Sahi and Puri have been involved with the ceremonial ritual performed in honour of Lord Jagannath on the occasion of the Snana Purnima in the lunar month of *Jyestha* (May-June). According to tradition on this day, Lord Jagannath, his sister Subhadra and elder brother Balabhadra are taken for a bath in the extremely cold water of the temple well as a result of which they fall ill; for the next 15 days they are kept in the Anasara Mandir and are given medicines to recover from the attack of flu. During this period, on the *singhasana* inside the main temple, three *pata* or images, painted by *chitrakaras* are placed. On another occasion, at the time of the Ratha Yatra during the lunar month of *Asadha* (June-July) the *chitrakaras* are called to execute colourful paintings on the three wooden chariots which carry the two divine brothers and their sister from the temple to their aunt's abode, where they remain for nine days.

Apart from their participation in these rituals the main source of income of the *chitrakaras* used to be from the sale of artefacts mainly in two places: at the Bedha Mahal inside the temple premises and in the Chakada Mahal just outside the main gate, near the Aruna pillar. These sites were auctioned to the highest bidder by the temple authorities. Generally the bidders would be from the trading community who would buy *pata chitras* from the *chitrakaras* and sell at a profit. At the beginning of the twentieth century, a certain Ananda Mohanty was the lease-holder of the Mahal and the chief middleman who would buy *pata chitra* from the *chitrakaras*. From time to time he would go to Raghurajpur with a cartload of paddy and rice and collect paintings in exchange of grains; those in urgent need would sell their paintings at a very cheap price. He would also provide cash loans against a bond promising to supply a specified number of paintings. Later he would falsify the papers claiming that the *chitrakaras* owed him hundreds of rupees and file suits for recovery of the money. By the late thirties most of the houses in Raghurajpur were owned by him. By the late fifties only a few old men among the 90-odd *chitrakara* families of Raghurajpur were still painting whereas all the youths had deserted the profession; it was only around the year 1953 that, with the intervention of an American lady, Mrs Halina Zealey, a new future opened up and the artists once again took out their brushes and colours.

Chintamani did not take long to reach a decision regarding Kelucharan's future; he had already sent his two elder sons, Ganesha and Ekadasi, to the Ras Leela troupe of Mohansundar Dev Goswami in Puri and in a few years they had returned having learnt to act and play the dhol and were now able to earn some money by performing in the different Jatra groups. Besides, he had a high opinion of Ras Leela as a performing art; it had an emotional impact on him, he would be moved to tears whenever he had watched it. He despised the *gotipua* performances for their cheapness and vulgarity, and appreciated the sober and deep devotional undercurrent which gave Ras Leela its peculiar flavour.

Hardly a fortnight had passed since the fateful day when Kelucharan had been forbidden to go to the *akhada* and he was handed over by his father to Mohansundar Goswami with the understanding that the child would remain with the guru for an extended period at his (Goswami's) expense and that a certain amount of money would be sent home periodically as his salary.

AWAY FROM HOME

WHEN Kelucharan joined the household of Mohansundar Goswami in Puri, he was a cute nine-year old boy with long curly hair, vivacious intelligent eyes and an insatiable thirst for learning. Apart from Goswami's family, consisting of his wife and son Gourasundar Dev, about 30 other children, between the ages of 8 and 18 years, were living in the house on Marichikot lane, all of whom were subjected to a strict and disciplined daily routine.

Guru Mohansundar Dev, born in the year 1892, was at that time in his forties; he was the twelfth descendant in a line directly deriving from Nityananda Mahaprabhu. The Goswamis originally belonged to Kharda in West Bengal and had settled down in Puri most probably since the time of Chaitanya in the sixteenth century. Nityananda Mahaprabhu was the *Karna Guru* of the Puri Maharaja and the *Gundicha Marjana Seva* (stone washing ceremony of Lord Jagannath's seat one day before the Ratha Yatra) was assigned to the Goswami family during the reign of King Prataparudradeva and this ritual is still carried on by them. It seems that the land in Raghurajpur where Sri Gouranga Mandir is located, was granted to the Goswamis by the same king for worshipping Chaitanya Mahaprabhu.

Mohansundar Dev lost his mother when he was two years old and his father, Haridev Goswami, when he was eight. From his unpublished diary, which is in the possession of his grandson Baturaj Dev, we find that his elder brother and sister took care of him until he was 11 and then he was left to fend for himself. He left his paternal house and stayed for about a year in the Pathara Akhada in Puri where he learnt to play the khol; at the age of 12 he left for Vrindavan and received the blessings of Lord Brindavaneswara. Five years later Mohansundar Dev returned to Puri; at the age of 17 he brought together some *sevayat* and travelled with these servitors all over Orissa performing Ras Sankirtana and Pranta Nataka (street plays) based on episodes from the Radha-Krishna story. He continued with these performances for about three years and then moved on to Nawadeep where he met Biswarupa Goswami, who was well known all over West Bengal for his performances of Ras Leela and Harinam Sankirtana. It was from Biswarupa Goswami that Mohansundar learnt to play the dhrupad pakhawaj, Hindustani singing, acting and stagecraft. And by performing as a member of Biswarupa's troupe all over Bengal, Mohansundar acquired a reputation both as an actor and musician. Back in Puri in 1918 he founded his own group known as the Radha Krishna Bihari Ras Party which ten years later was renamed as Sri Radha Kunjabihari Ras Party. Soon Mohansundar became a legendary figure in Orissa.

The house which Kelucharan came to live in, had been

The small shrine in Mohansundar Dev Goswami's house, with the idols of Kunjabihari and Radharani in the centre.

built by Mohansundar between 1920 and 1925 with financial help from the head of the Emarmatha of Puri, Mahanta Maharaja. It had a spacious hall in the front (12 X 50 ft) with pressed cow dung flooring and a straw roof (*chala ghara*), which was separated from the rest of the house by a small courtyard where a big *champa* tree stood in the middle and on one side was the shrine of the family deity. The main portion of the house was three-storeyed having the main bedroom on the first floor and a small cubicle for the guru's meditation on the top floor. The cooking and washing area at the back was enclosed by plants and trees.

Children were selected by Mohansundar Dev on the basis of their talent for singing or acting; at times they came from one particular village from where other children had already been selected or were discovered by the guru during his frequent tours giving performances. The students lived together, most of them slept in the *chala ghara* and some, who had important roles, around the guru's bed on the first floor. The daily routine began early in the morning with the singing practice of the basic notes in music *sa re ga ma pa dha ni sa* and the songs from the *Gita Govinda* or the Vaishnava poems. Such a practice was considered an important aspect of the training since the children had to sing while portraying the different roles on stage and the performances being held in the open air and without any amplification system, the voice had to be properly trained and developed. The morning singing classes were personally supervised by the guru and the boys were asked to memorize the songs and, whoever was able to write, had to pen them down in his notebook.

Mohansundar Dev Goswami.

At the beginning of a Ras performance, Mohansundar would deliver a lecture on tenets of the Vaishnava philosophy and intersperse it with songs. Although fragile in appearance, he had a powerful voice capable of holding the attention of large audiences, as large as 4,000 to 5,000 people. He was an excellent orator and singer and was able to address the assembled public in terms which could be easily undestood by them; he explained concepts such as the inter-relation between the *atman-paramatman* (individual-universal soul), mind-body, the five elements in the formation of the material universe, *maya* (illusion) and *brahaman* (reality), with comparisons and images directly drawn from everyday experiences of the common man. This basic method of understanding and explaining theoretical concepts with the help of examples from a practical and accessible field of experience is a characteristic trait of Kelucharan's approach to life. The ten years that he spent in close contact with such an eclectic personality left an indelible mark on him.

Mohansundar Dev was also a distinguished singer; in 1933 seven of his songs, written, set to music and sung by him, were recorded by the HMV studio in Calcutta. The theme of these songs, as of most of the librettos of the dance-dramas written by him, was again that of his beloved Krishna, his playful games and mischievous pranks, his infinite bliss and compassion; some of them, like '*Asa bhai luchakali kheliba*' (come brother, let's play hide and seek) and '*Aha mo Nanda kole Govinda*' (aha, how beautiful is my Govinda sitting in the lap of Nanda) became popular Oriya devotional songs.

The day proceeded with rehearsals which began immediately after having taken *prasadam* (strictly vegetarian food offered first to the family deity and then taken by the entire household) and continued up to 11 a.m. The casting in the dance-dramas was done by the guru and each boy was taught how to act, sing, move around, and gesticulate depending upon the character assigned to him. Rehearsals were conducted till the puja *bhog*, when the entire group sang the '*Hari nam kirtana*' in front of the small temple in the courtyard of the house. The same routine was followed in the afternoon with the rehearsals being conducted at the *chala ghara* until the time of the *sandhya arati* (evening offer of light to the deity) when evening *kirtana* with the accompaniment of khol and cymbals was sung before the deities.

Kunjabihari and Radharani were the two idols that were worshipped in the Goswami household; the first one had been brought to Puri by some devotees from Nagaland who had come at the time of the Ratha Yatra and spent the night in the courtyard of Haridev Goswami's house. That night Lord Krishna visited him in his dreams and announced his arrival at Haridev's house and wanted to be worshipped there. The next morning Mohansundar's father, Haridev, collected the *murti* from the Nagas and built a small temple in a corner of the courtyard where it has remained till today. While the Kunjabihari idol was in stone, the one of Radharani was made of *ashtadhatu* (eight different metals); this was donated by the king of Puri and was installed by the side of Lord Krishna after completion of their marriage ceremony.

The atmosphere in the house was so charged with the divine love of Radha and Krishna that no action, word or thought seemed to exist outside this world; children were brought up in an atmosphere of devotion and discipline which permeated their lives as well as their art. Body and mind grew attuned to this mystical reality, with no discrepancy between the world of man and the realm of God. The first thing Kelucharan had to do on joining this group was to shave his long curly hair and discard the ornaments which were part of his *gotipua* past: the silver four-faced bracelets, and nose and earrings were substituted by a simple *tulsi mala* (*tulsi* bead necklace) which was first consecrated to the deities and then offered by the guru to each disciple.

His first step as an actor was performing the role of *bala* Krishna (little Krishna) in the play *Balya Leela* (Child Play). He had to sing the song '*Asa bhai luchakali kheliba*' while playing with his other friends, the shepherds of Vrindavan, and his first cue was to mother Jasodha, asking her why she had not brought him the little yellow bird which she had promised him the previous day. The children were assigned roles according to their age and, of course, talent; the character of *bala* Krishna depicted little Krishna up to the age of 12, followed by Madana Mohana which covered the Krishna story up to the age of 20. The role of the adult Krishna, first as the king of Dwaraka and later as a guide and intermediary in the Kurukshetra war, was not portrayed in the Ras Leela but was included in the *nataka* or dramatic plays, where acting and dialogue were more important than singing.

Although most of the members of the troupe were male, who performed both female and male roles, two girls had been accepted as part of the community: Radharani—the daugther of a *mahari's* sister—who portrayed the character of Brundadevi, and Bidhyutlata Mohanty—the daughter of a prostitute—who specialized in the role of Chandrabali. But the most memorable female roles were portrayed by two male members of the troupe; the role of Radha was depicted by a boy named Basudeva and that of Lalita by Raghunatha Nanda, who had been selected by Mohansundar when he heard him sing along with his father at the Bada Danda (main road of Puri). Both the roles were quite demanding; while the first one was more intense and introverted, the second was said to be full of humour and wit, and it seems that Raghunatha was so good in portraying this humorous character that he would get medals for the role every time he performed it.

Kelucharan had performed the role of *bala* Krishna for about four months when Biswarupa Goswami, Mohansudar Dev's guru, came to Puri on his annual visit. And this happened to be at the time of *Gundicha Marjana*. This ritual has been performed by the Goswami family ever since the Rath Yatra began to be held. Kelucharan remembers him as a huge sadhu, 7 ft tall with a plait of hair—12 hands long—which he used to wind over the head in two layers pinned with two gold hairpins. He had such a powerful voice that whenever he sang '*Shambu Shiva hara hara trinayana jata dhari*' (salutation to Shiva, who has three eyes and wears matted hairs) playing the dhrupad pakhawaj himself, the window-panes of the house would shake. Due to his yogic powers he could eat for ten people as well as fast for ten days consecutively.

One day he took the children with him to the Narendra Tank for his morning bath. Suddenly, he disappeared under water only to reappear after a while, floating like a dead body. He remained in that condition for seven days until on the eighth day, while the children were bathing all around, with a sudden move he seized Kelucharan's legs from below making him jump out of fear. The children were overjoyed to see him alive once again. He would make Kelucharan sit on his stomach and seize the child in mid-air after throwing him up in the air with a jerk. He was fond of all children, but he had a soft corner for little Kelucharan after he saw him play the role of *bala* Krishna. During that very first visit, before leaving Puri, he took the child to one side and told Mohansundar never to beat him for any reason. And from that day onward Kelucharan occupied a special place in Mohansundar's heart.

Kelucharan returned home for the first time for a holiday after spending three or four years with the Ras Leela troupe. About a week after his return, one afternoon his father while polishing a *poti* with the *chikana* stone, noticed that Kelucharan was going out holding a little box and asked him what he was up to. Kelucharan had 40 pieces of paper in the box with the numbers and symbols of playing cards written on them. On hearing that he was going to play cards, his father raised his hand and threatened to fling the *chikana* stone at him. As his elder son Ganesha was squandering large sums of money because of his addiction to the game of cards, Kelucharan's father could not bear the thought of another of his son falling prey to the same vice.

Taken aback by his father's violent reaction, Kelucharan at once emptied the contents of the box, mentally bowed to the family elders by touching the door post with his head. He ran crying to say goodbye to his mother, who was offering prayers in front of the Bhuasuni Temple and walked towards Puri, straight to his guru's house. He covered the distance of about 12 km in barely one hour. It was summer time and all the other children had gone back to their villages. It took quite some time before Mohansundar could get out of Kelucharan details of the incident. On hearing that little Kelu's father had threatened to beat him Mohansundar got angry as he could not tolerate anybody being violent with Kelucharan. When Chintamani arrived to enquire about his son the same evening, Mohansundar told him straightaway that now Kelucharan was 'his son' and Chintamani had no right over him. Chintamani replied that he had just come to find out if the child had reached safely, and quietly returned to his village. Kelucharan did not return to Raghurajpur until his father was alive. Once in a while the latter would come to collect money (towards the boy's salary) from the guru or visit the ashram with his wife to get a glimpse of his son performing the Ras Leela.

Kelucharan was more than a son to his guru; he, along with another child, were the only ones who would be allowed to do such *seva* to him as anointing his body with oil, giving him a massage, preparing the water for his daily bath and bathing him. Later, when the guru contracted a disease similar to leprosy—his entire body was covered all over with boils and cysts—only Kelucharan took constant care of him by cleaning him, applying the *chal mugra* oil and helping him in all his daily needs. Mohansundar suffered terribly due to this illness; he believed that he was being punished for attempting to spread the '*nigudha keli rahasya*' (secret love play) of Radha and Krishna among all and sundry.

Besides the personal *seva* to Mohansundar, other housework kept Kelucharan busy; he would be the first to get up at dawn and call the boys for the morning singing class, and between the classes and rehearsals would find time for sweeping the floor, washing dishes and helping his guru's wife in other domestic chores. There was no other servant in the house except for a Brahmin who did the cooking. By the time the Raghurajpur episode took place, Kelucharan had advanced in his career as a Ras Leela actor having performed all the preliminary roles of *bala* Krishna, *ashta gopi* (eight types of friends who serve Radha and Krishna in their love play), Bisakha and Lalita (two of Radha's best friends). After having performed the role of Radha for about five to six months, he changed over to playing the role of Krishna until he was eighteen.

The boys remained indoors in Puri for two to three months during the rainy season, and it was during this period that plays were rehearsed and training was given to the recruits in their respective roles. Besides the summer months which were a time to rest, the remainder of the year the troupe performed all over Orissa and also at times in the adjacent states. They would travel by all available modes of transport: bus, truck, bullock cart, cycle rickshaw, train and at times even on foot, lugging the musical instruments and sets required for the show. The troupe usually consisted of 50 to 60 members; after reaching the place and having settled down at the local *dharamshala,* they would start the work of raising a platform. The stage which was made with excavated earth was usually 2.5 ft high, 20 ft long and 18 ft wide. Spectators would sit in the pit dug all around the stage. This would be covered by a *chamundia* (roof) made of intertwined bamboo strips and coconut leaves.

During those days a Ras Leela performance by Mohansundar's troupe would easily attract an audience of 3,000 to 4,000 which would include not only residents from the village where the performance took place but also even those living miles away. Some of the plays, although dramatized and directed by him, were not fully composed by him but were drawn from lyrics by several Vaishnava poets of Orissa. The selection of lyrics would depend on the plot of a particualr play. As a result of which lyrics from Jayadeva, Banamali, Baladeva Ratha, Upendra Bhanja and other Oriya poets were included in the libretto of some of his most frequently staged plays such as *Vidagdha Madhava* (The clever husband of the Mother Goddess), *Vidagdha Chintamani* (The clever wish fulfiller), *Mathura Mangala* (Joy of Mathura), *Sri Radhapremamruta* (Radha's nectar of love), *Mana Bhanjana* (assuaging her pretended anger), *Sudama*

Daridra Bhanjana (Remover of Sudama's poverty), *Ghostha Chandrama* (Moon of cowherds) and *Bilwa Mangala*.

The plays that were fully written by Mohansundar include: *Ananda Brundavana Champu* (The bliss of Vrindavana), *Adharamruta* (The nectar of lips), *Sarata Rasa* (Autumn), *Sri Gobinda Lilamruta* (The sweet sports of Gobinda) and *Abhisara* (Going towards the tryst). Apart from some of his poetry collections which were published in the years 1929-30 most of his other works still remain unpublished.

In a Ras Leela play the musical score and the songs sung by the actors were given priority; few lines of recitation were interspersed just to create pauses or links between sequences. The orchestra was conducted by Mohansundar, who accompanied himself on the harmonium; the other instruments in the orchestra were a khol and a manjira (cymbals). During performances in Puri, at times a flautist and a sitarist would also join the team. The stage setting was simple and rustic; the performances relied more on an emotional impact than on a spectacular one. Three curtains hung from the top bamboo structure and two wings on the sides provided the stage backdrop and delimitation; on the front curtain Radha and Krishna were depicted in amourous dalliance. At the beginning of the play, standing in front of the curtain, Mohansundar would deliver a lecture on the Vaishnava philosophy of life. His lectures and songs were meant both for drawing people to the performance and introducing them to the spirit of Vaishnavism. Usually he would start either with a citation from the *Gita Govinda* or with a song; one of these songs is still recited by Kelucharan every evening during his daily prayers:

Bande chandraka charu sikandaka gobardhana giridhari,
ghatana kalebara natana sundara puta hataka kara,
kankana suruchira thani bhanana dhara,
gopi pattahara Madhu Kaitabha danujari.

I salute him, who wears a peacock feather on his forehead and who raised the Gobardhana mountain, whose body is beautiful, who dances beautifully with golden bangles on his hands, who stole the clothes of the gopi, the slayer of Madhu and Kaitabha.

Tickets for these performances were sold at the nominal price of 4 and 8 *annas*. With the opening of the first curtain, all the actors would be standing in line holding a small branch of the *tulsi* plant and a *pata chitra* of Radha and

Krishna; the backdrop for this introductory scene was a painted curtain depicting a road in perspective. After singing the *vandana* or invocatory Sanskrit *sloka* (which varied from play to play), the actors would place their offerings of *tulsi* and *pata chitra* on the stage and walk away. After the third painted curtain appeared the play would begin. On this curtain the scene depicted was that of the luxurious ambience of Vrindavan, with one big *kadamba* tree in the middle. Real branches of trees and flower decorations on both sides of the wings were used to add richness to the scene. Kunja Maharana from Raghurajpur was incharge of setting the stage, and the curtains were painted by Krishna Mukherjee of Puri.

In the Ras Leela style of recitation, hand gestures, eye movements, inclination of the head, facial expressions were determined by the context of the particular song which the artists were meant to render. The emphasis was not as much on the stylization of movements as on the emotional charge conveyed by the chosen attitude. Gestures used by the actors were taken from daily life and while acting they held real objects such as garlands, bangles, handkerchiefs, etc., according to the requirement. The foot movements in the dance were minimal. According to the basic combinations the steps ranged from one to six. These steps were usually employed in the last scene of a play where the union of Radha and Krishna was celebrated by all the gopis in a dance performed in a circle. Arm in arm, they performed a dance the purpose of which would be more for displaying devotional abandon than technical skill.

For the rest of the play the actors would mostly move around, addressing each other through songs and gestures concentrating on the intensity of the mood to be conveyed. The *satwika* aspect was given the maximum importance; Guru Goswami would instruct the children from the wings, to help them concentrate and identify completely with the situation. Tears were supposed to be real, and Kelucharan remembers having really fainted on the stage when, as Krishna, he asked Radha for forgiveness in the famous sequence of '*dehi pada pallavamudaram*' (place your foot on my head) from the nineteenth song of the *Gita Govinda*. While composing the same scene many years later, in 1981, Kelucharan made the dancer portraying Krishna repeat that particular gesture of submission 21 times during a rehearsal, and yet was not satisfied with the result.

The audience at these performances usually responded with great enthusiasm and emotional intensity. The audience was familiar with the texts of the songs and, hence, the eternal story of the divine lovers enacted in front of their eyes would reach out to their hearts and enable them to participate in the performance.

One of the most successful plays directed by Goswami was *Mana Bhanjana*, which include besides his own songs, poems from Jayadeva, Gopalakrishna and Banamali.

The *vandana* or initial *sloka* for this play is '*Srita kamala kucha mandala*' (you rest on the circle of Sri's breast) from the second song of the *Gita Govinda*, after which Radha, offended and dejected, appears surrounded by her gopis. She is annoyed with Krishna and refuses to wear anything black—dress or ornaments; she asks Lalita to remove all dark objects from her sight as they remind her of her unfaithful lover. Her friends tease her: 'How will you eliminate the darkness which embraces you when you close your eyes?' 'I'll bite a diamond and commit suicide', she replies.

In the following scene Krishna in connivance with Lalita, tries to approach Radha under different disguises; these were enacted by the actor by quickly wrapping himself up in different cloths in the brief period of time at his disposal between appearances on the stage (Kelucharan adopted the same trick when in recent years he played Ravana in the *Ramayana* dance-drama and had to approach Sita disguised as a mendicant).

In his first disguise as *maluni* or garland vendor he is rejected by Radha after she discovers that one of the leaves bears the name of Krishna; next he reappears as *napituni*, the woman who goes from house-to-house to give a pedicure and apply *alata* or red liquid on the feet. Although well received at first, she is immediately sent away when she tries to write the name of Krishna under Radha's feet. In the next disguise he appears as *kachara* or the bangle seller but again he is thrown out when he tries to sell a black bangle.

Lalita at this point informs Radha of the arrival of a handsome sadhu or mendicant at their door who insists on receiving alms from a *pativrata* as it would increase his yogic powers. The word '*pativrata*' literally means a woman devoted to her husband but in this case refers to Radha who, although married to Chandasena, had not consummated her marriage. The word thus signified a 'pure' and 'chaste' woman. While giving him alms their eyes meet and Radha goes into a trance. After his departure, she recognizes the conch and the lotus marks in the footprints left behind and a tear falls from her eyes (a real tear is supposed to fall on one of Krishna's footprint). Unable to bear the separation any longer she sends Lalita to fetch Krishna, but at this point Brundavati comes on the stage and announces that Krishna must have drowned in the river since his peacock feather and *mukuta* were found on the river bank. On receiving this news Radha disappears as if drawn into the dark waters of the Yamuna.

In the last scene, the two divine lovers appear embracing each other; a swing is lowered on the stage from the top and sitting on the swing they are pushed by the *sakhis* while the Rasa dance is performed. At the end of the performance the audience would throng around Radha and Krishna and compete with each other to get a few flowers from the *gajara* or garlands worn by them. Krishna's garland would consist of three types of flowers: *ketaki*, *tarata* and *malli*. Kelucharan remembers how, after each performance in Puri, the two daughters of Kshetramani Mohanty, the Superintendent of Police of Puri, would always be the first to snatch the garlands from his neck.

The variety of songs included in these plays gave ample scope to Kelucharan to familiarize himself with myriads of little episodes and details which form part of the imaginative and rich Oriya literature around the mythical story of Radha and Krishna in the sixteenth and seventeenth centuries. Not only did he imbibe from this experience the knowledge of the content and meaning of the songs but also the *bhakti bhava* or the devotional quality in them. In the later years, in his famous dance compositions of Jayadeva's *ashtapadi* many of these elements were included to form the *sanchari* or elaborations on the main theme, and his highly aesthetic renditions of the erotic content of the poems were sustained by an undercurrent of *bhakti* which prevented them from becoming cheap or vulgar.

Kelucharan was so drawn into this mystic reality of the world that one day, along with Raghunath Nanda, the naughty Lalita, he set forth on foot towards the mythic Vrindavan, the land of Sri Krishna.

On reaching the Puri railway station the two boarded

the first train which they found standing on the platform when a suspicious ticket collector approached them asking for their tickets. After hearing that they did not have any money with them, he asked what their destination was. When told that they wanted to reach the land of Sri Krishna, he politely requested them to alight and wait at the platform since that train was going in the opposite direction. He sent word to Mohansundar Goswami and immediately Agadhu Maharana, the khol player from Raghurajpur, came and brought back the two fugitives.

Temple dedicated to goddess Bhuasuni, under construction at Raghurajpur.

Years later, in 1998, Kelucharan was to run away in a similar fashion, this time not towards Vrindavan but towards his 'mother' Bhuasuni, the goddess to whom he had been offered as a child when he was three years old. Almost in a frenzy, with a *gamcha* on his shoulder and no money in his pocket, one late afternoon, frustrated in his attempts to console his wife who had suddenly burst into tears for no apparent reason, he left his house on foot and using public transport reached Raghurajpur and took shelter under the huge banyan tree near the vermilion smeared face of the goddess. By this time Kelucharan has become a cult figure in the field of dance, with hundreds of admirers and students scattered all over the globe. His name is synonymous with Odissi dance and is considered one of the greatest performing artists India has ever produced. His return to the village goddess at the base of the large banyan tree that day marked the beginning of his last project in life: construction of a temple dedicated to the goddess Bhuasuni his beloved 'mother'. On this occasion his wife and son had to bring him back from his mystic trip.

It was during a performance at Kendrapada in Orissa that a telegram carrying the news of his father's demise reached him. Kelucharan was at that time about 15 years old. Mohansundar Goswami had received the telegram when the Ras Leela show was on; at the end of it Kelucharan came as usual to do *pranam* to the guru and found him sitting with his head bent as if engrossed in thought. The boy asked him if he would like to have a massage and the guru in turn asked what he meant to him. Kelucharan replied that he was more than a father to him. Goswami asked him to remove his make-up and the costume of Krishna and have some food. After dinner he showed him the telegram; Kelucharan could not control himself, and burst into tears.

It was the last show of the season and after packing all their belongings they waited for a vehicle which would take them to Cuttack.

Petrol was scarce in those days on account of the impending Second World War. The passenger train from Cuttack to Puri used to halt briefly at Janakadeipur station from where Goswami sent a message to Kelucharan's mother through a person known to them. Although the boy was already 15 years old, Goswami would never let him go alone anywhere. This reminds me of the same over-protective attitude Kelucharan had later on towards students residing at his house during the summer workshops: nobody would ever be allowed to leave the house without an escort!

Siri Nani reached Puri the same evening and tearfully conveyed to her son his father's last advice to him:

hate mapi chakhande chala (before proceeding measure the road);
karaja karibu ni, karma kara (don't run into debts, perform your duty);
jou rastare mu rakhili, sethire mora nama rakha (acquire fame in the field where I placed you).

Kelucharan receiving the Padma Bhushan award in March 1988.

His mother remembered these last words when in 1988, about 45 years later, Kelucharan placed at her feet the Padma Bhushan citation, which he received from the Goverment of India!

'I will tell your father what you have achieved when I meet him in heaven', she told him with tears in her eyes.

Since it was vacation time, Kelucharan took leave of his guru, and for the first time after the playing cards incident, he went back with his mother to the village. His father's cremation had already been performed; he paid homage to his father by visiting and touching the site where the body had been burnt, and made a promise that he will fulfil his father's desires. From then on his visits to the village became more frequent as he found himself more at ease whenever he was there.

Since 1937, performances by Mohansundar Goswami's troupe had become irregular due to the guru's ill health and financial problems, and quite often during the course of the year the children were sent to their respective villages for brief periods. Even so Kelucharan always preferred to remain at his side, going back home only when absolutely necessary.

In 1936, Goswami produced the first Oriya film, *Sita Bibaha* (Sita's marriage), based on a play written by Kamapala Misra. It was released in the month of April at the Laxmi Cinema Hall of Puri. Although he received substantial guidance and advice in this venture from the Kali Films Studio of Calcutta, in order to raise Rs. 30,000 to meet the cost of the film, Goswami had to mortgage all his property (including the house in Puri, which would be retrieved only in the early nineties by his grandson Bataraj Dev Goswami). As a result he found himself under severe financial constraints, and often appealed for help from the different religious heads of Puri.

However, the film was a success and brought Goswami a great deal of fame. By playing the role of Viswamitra, he demonstrated once more his versatility as an artist. Among the other favourite roles that he interpreted on stage were those of Sudama and Bilwa Mangala. For Kelucharan it was always a valuable experience to be able to watch his guru in these roles and when he was about 17 years old he got an opportunity to perform the role of Sudama in the play *Sudama Daridra Bhanjana* (Remover of Sudama's poverty).

The story revolves around the poor Brahmin Sudama and his search for his childhood friend Krishna, who had become the powerful king of Dwaraka. Sudama's simple and child-like devotion, his single-mindedness and undemanding loyalty, the comic overtones and popular appeal, are all characteristics which in the late eighties Kelucharan would transfer to the interpretation of another role which can be described as the best in his entire career, the role of the boatman Kaibata in the well-known episode from the *Ramayana* where Rama requested to be ferried across the river Ganga on his way to the Panchavati forest.

Another of Kelucharan's talents which was discovered during this period was his outstanding capacity for interpreting female roles. Mohansundar wanted to cast him in the role of Sita in the *Ramayana*, but since Kelucharan was already eighteen years old, his guru wanted to be sure whether at that age he could still be feminine enough in his portrayal of this character. On being asked to demonstrate his special talent, Kelucharan imitated the gait and posture of a woman coming back from the river carrying a pot full of water on her hips. The imitation was so accurate that Goswami could not believe his eyes; he had never taught that particular feat to him and wondered how the boy could have learnt it. Kelucharan told him that as a small child he had observed his mother along with her two sisters-in-law walking in that fashion and covering their faces whenever they passed in front of their respective husbands sitting on the doorstep. It was that image, still fresh in his mind, which he was imitating. Similarly Kelucharan used to astonish all of us in the class by his accurate imitation of the gait and mannerisms of his students.

Had Kelucharan gone beyond the need of having a master? Important changes in life are often determined by small incidents the significance of which can only be understood when seen in retrospect. He had learnt a lot and in return given a lot during those ten years; it is difficult to assess which one was more. From the very beginning he had been indispensable to his guru; the latter would not let himself be washed or fed by anybody other than Kelucharan. At the peak of his illness, when his entire body was covered with cysts and filled with pus, only Kelucharan would take care of him—washing him, massaging him and even helping him to the toilet. He was more than a son to his master;

Goswami was often heard repeating this even in front of his own son and wife, and this may have led to slight jealousy on their part.

On a fateful day a certain Jai Makadama, a zamindar friend of Mohansundar Goswami, had come to pay a visit to him and had brought with him a lot of paddy and vegetables as gift. While offering all this to Goswami's wife, he also handed over some gold for safe custody which at a later date he would collect from her. Since Kelucharan was the custodian of all the house keys he was asked to store the vegetables and other things in the store room and to place the gold in the almirah of the first floor bedroom.

That same evening Kelucharan had planned to see a new movie released at the Laxmi Cinema Hall; the picture was *Kangan* and had Leela Chitnis and Ashok Kumar in the leading roles. He had been to a cinema hall only twice until now, and on both occasions along with his guru to see the picture *Sita Bibaha*. The medium had fascinated him from the very instant he saw the first images projected on to the big screen; he was attracted by the decor, the recitation of the actors, the dramatic twists in the story and above all by the possibility of studying the characters and learning more about the histrionic art. Fascination for this medium was to remain with him even in later years. When in the early eighties he was in a position to buy a television set, one could find him glued to it for hours together.

After having told his friend Basudeva, the one who used to do the role of Radha, that if Goswami searched for him, he should be told that he had gone to sleep in the *chala ghara* along with the other boys, Kelucharan left the house around 9.15 p.m. to be in time for the last show of the film. Towards midnight, Mohansundar got up from his bed and looked all over for the young student and in the process woke up the whole household. Kelucharan was nowhere to be found. Guruma, Goswami's wife, had a suspicion: was it possible that Kelucharan had run away with the gold? Without consulting her husband, she immediately sent her son to the police station to file a case against Kelucharan. The Superintendent of Police of Puri, Kshetramani Mohanty never believed him; he and his two daughters were among the most devoted fans of Kelucharan and it was simply impossible for them to imagine that their 'Krishna' was a thief.

On Gourasundar Dev's return, his father scolded him

for having gone to the police station without first verifying the facts; it was at this point that Kelucharan reached the courtyard of the house. He was standing under the big *chandana* tree when he overheard his guru abusing his (Kelucharan's) mother; he was startled and the keys fell from his hands. As a result Mohansundar's wife knew that Kelucharan was around; Gourasundar came down and saw Kelucharan and the flow of people passing outside. He informed his father that Kelu had gone to see a film. Kelucharan picked up the keys, deposited them at Guruma's feet and went to sit on the doorstep of the house, facing the main road.

The whole household went back to sleep while he sat there until the next day; a man from his village passed by, he sent word through him to his mother to come and fetch him. A policeman informed him about the allegations that had been made against him at the police station the previous night. Kelucharan listened unperturbed; he had already decided on his next step.

That day, after everybody had had their food, he entered the house to collect some money from his savings; with it he went to a nearby hotel to eat meat (something absolutely forbidden in the purely vegetarian diet of the Goswami household). When his mother arrived, he was still sitting on the doorstep; he asked her to take him back home. He went in to offer *pranam* to his guru and his wife; both of them tried to dissuade him from going away but he said that since he had lost their trust he could not remain with them anymore. His guru in a fit of anger cursed him: 'Are you leaving me in this condition? Go if you have to, but you will also face what I am facing today!'

Outside the house he asked his mother for a rupee and saw the film *Kangan* once more. After spending the night in a relative's house, the next day they set out for home on foot. While they were still on the road the train from Puri overtook them; Kelucharan spotted some of his ashram friends in the train. On reaching the village they told him that after his departure that day Goswami did not allow anybody to help him and had sent all the boys back to their homes. Kelucharan was stunned on hearing that Mohansundar had wound up the Ras Leela group because he had left him

After a few years, in 1947, Gourasundar saw Kelucharan performing the *Dashavatara* at the Annapurna A Group in Puri and told his father that the teenager had become an excellent dancer. Mohansundar sent for Kelucharan. His illness was in a very advanced state. He showed the boy his hands fully covered in sores and told him: 'See, after you went away nobody took care of me anymore. But you have done what you had to do; I take away from you any evil. May you proceed on your life's journey with my blessings. Come and be one of my pall-bearers after my death.'

Mohansundar Dev spent the last days of his life in great agony; in his last song he addressed his motherland Orissa:

> O my motherland, Orissa, I am taking leave of you. I ask for your blessings so that my life will be spent in singing the old devotional songs of Orissa up to my death and again, at the end of my journey the stream of my life has dried up. The messengers of death are now piping at me from the cremation ground. The body has become weak; diseases are taking revenge on me.

On his death bed, before dying, he was blessed with the *darshana* of his beloved deities; he called Gourasundar's wife and told her: 'Don't you see, Radha and Krishna have entered the house. Why don't you get a seat for them?'

After that he drank the *paduka* (sacred water from the deities' bath) and blessed his two grandchildren with it. Before dying he expressed three desires: that a mandir should be built on the land given to them for *seva*. That his son should carry on with the performance of Ras Leela and that one of his grandchildren should carry on the *seva* of Lord Jagannath and Lord Kunjabihari. His son Gourasundar reviewed the activities of the Rasa party in Puri in the early fifties under the name of Mohan Theatres, and to date, his grandson Bataraj Dev still continues the *seva* to the deities.

It was the month of January and the year was 1948. Kelucharan learnt of his guru's death three days after the tragedy and, therefore, could not be a pall-bearer. The memory of his beloved master inspired him all his life. From that day onwards the guru's name has always been among the first to be remembered by Kelucharan in his daily puja to Lord Jagannath.

ODD JOBS

As long as Kelucharan was a member of the Ras Leela troupe, the hardships of the wartime did not affect him much. Apart from the occasional drill, military planes flying in the sky, and having to endure at times food and petrol scarcity, the daily life of the group proceeded undisturbed.

But when Kelucharan left his guru's ashram in 1943 and came back to his village, the situation was quite grim. Hardly any *chitrakara* family in the village was able to pursue the trade; scarcity of food, jobs and lack of money had hit everyone hard. People had already mortgaged whatever they had without being able to improve their economic condition. Labour contractors would come every morning to hire the healthiest men from the village for a meagre wage of 15-20 *paisa* a day, hardly sufficient at a time when prices of essential commodities were sky-rocketing.

Few days after his return, Kelucharan's elder brother Ekadasi suggested that he start working in the *panna baraja* (betel leaf fields) like many others in the village. These plantations are a common sight even today in the areas around Raghurajpur and Chandanpur, as the region has the ideal soil and the right degree of humidity for growing betel leaf. The betel is a creeper which grows only in the shade, protected from extreme heat and cold; the rows of betel plants are lined at a distance of 4 ft from each other and the *baraja* or plantation is protected on the top and the four sides by mats made of bamboo strips interlaced with *chamundia* (coconut leaves). They need constant watering and a constant induction of fresh soil. The tip of each plant is brought down near the roots and replanted nine times before a plantation is abandoned and a new one is started nearby. Due to this constant increase in soil level, a *panna baraja* comes to resemble a small hill surrounded by a trench, situated in the vicinity of a pool.

Work in a betel plantation includes a variety of activities and the terminology used to describe them is peculiar to this plantation: *kana chhinda* (to change the bamboo canes used as support to the creepers), *na ala* (to lower the upper portions of the plant), *goda bandha* (to roll the lowered portion around the bottom of the cane), *kuta bachha* (to clean the ground), *peti bandha* (to fix the middle portions of the creepers to the cane), and *panna loda* (to pull out the leaves). While describing all this, to make me understand, Kelucharan would mime these activities with extremely graceful hand gestures as if he was composing a dance on the theme. Only after I entered one of these enclosures and saw from close quarters the delicacy of the creepers did I realize how the dance did not need to be composed but was intrinsic to the actual work itself.

The atmosphere inside the enclosure has a magical quality about it; the light filtering through the *chamundia* and the freshness of the cool, shadowy interior, the neatly kept rows of creepers gives one the feeling of having been transported to some fairy-tale garden. It reminded me of the *mudra* used by Kelucharan in '*dhira samire Yamuna tire . . .*' (a soft breeze blows on the bank of the Yamuna) to describe how Krishna plucked the softest leaves to prepare a bed of flowers for Radha; the *mudra* and movement he had used to describe the plucking of leaves or *panna loda* was performed before my eyes by the old man working in the *baraja*. The leaves have to be plucked at the root of the stem with a circular movement of the hand by holding them between the thumb and index finger and then deposited in a fan-shaped pattern in a basket so that the rotten ones may be discarded. An equal amount of nimbleness is required in handling the soft tips of the creepers and in lowering them without damaging the plant.

The neatly intertwined *chamundia* over my head reminded me of the bamboo-made under-roof constructed by Kelucharan for the dancing hall of his house in Cuttack. Under its shade many dancers and choreographic masterpieces have come alive; perhaps a similar *chamundia* was used to protect the stage of a Ras Leela performance under which Kelucharan's talent as an actor and dancer had been nurtured.

The work in the *baraja* may not have appeared so poetical to Kelucharan at that time, especially because being a young lad he had to perform the most strenuous chores involved in the job such as carrying water from the pool to the *baraja* or depositing fresh soil at the roots of the plants. For a mere 20 *annas* a day he would have to carry up to 125 buckets of water climbing at times 25-30 steps from the pools to the raised level of the plantation!

In the evenings, after the day's grind, Kelucharan would spend time at the *akhada* run by Mohan Maharana, situated to the right of the Gopinath Temple. After the sudden departure of Balabhadra Sahu from the village, this was the only *akhada* left and served as a sort of evening meeting place for musicians, actors and *gotipua* dancers of Raghurajpur to exchange and share ideas. Kelucharan would share with others his knowledge of *abhinaya* acquired during his ten year apprenticeship with Mohansundar Goswami and in return he had access to the different combinations of rhythmic syllables used for playing the mardala. The main percussionist here was Agadhu Maharana who had also been the main khol player in Mohansundar's troupe.

On occasions Kelucharan would accompany his elder brother Ganesha when he played the mardala for *gotipua* troupes performing in some far-away village. Once, while we were travelling by car towards Raghurajpur, he described one of these trips in detail:

> We set on foot at about four o'clock in the morning from our village and we reached Pipli around 5 p.m., covering the entire distance of 30 miles with hardly any rest. My brother Ganesha was walking very fast and I was not able to keep pace with him. Whenever he would stop to roll a *bidi* or make a *pan* I would get a chance to slow down the pace, but he would catch up with me before long and I would have to start running again. We came along the railway track up to Sakhigopal and then took the main road. At this point I had my bath, in this very tank, and here under this banyan tree I stopped for a while unable to proceed further. On reaching our destination, my feet had swelled up so much that I had to sleep the entire night with my legs propped up on a window sill. We had two days of rehearsals before the show and then, the day after the performance, we walked back all the way home.

During this period Kelucharan learnt some basic *bols* or rhythmic sequences which in the late fifties, were moulded into the rhythmic structure of the *mangala charan* and *batu* presented in the Odissi dance. The sequences '*thari kita dhi dallanga ta tha*' or '*ta kadataka dhi kadataka ta dhi kadataka je kete taka je je nam ta tha*', for example, were already played to the accompaniment of the *gotipua* rendering of *nritta* or pure dance but without being set in any particular *tala* or division of beats. This work of systematization was carried on in the late fifties by a team of people involved in laying down the basic tenets of Odissi dance.

During his years of performance in the Ras Leela troupe Kelucharan had continued to practise on the percussion all through although until then the mardala, for which he was to become famous later on, had not yet become his chosen instrument. After having learnt the technique of playing the khol from his father and his uncle during his childhood, he continued playing the instrument under the tutelage of Agadhu Maharana and Mohansundar Goswami; during this period he also had his first lessons in tabla playing from Kshetramohan Kar, a renowned tabla ustad residing in Puri. He would visit the master at his residence, accompanied by Mohansundar Goswami to observe the fingers drumming and the technique demonstrated by him, but Kelucharan never had the courage to play before him. He would rehearse whatever he had seen only after returning to the ashram.

For the first 30 years of his life Kelucharan exercised his inborn sense of rhythm by playing both the khol and the tabla; it was only during the second phase of his life, with the emergence of Odissi dance in the early fifties, that he became adept at playing the mardala. He had no formal training in playing this instrument; he developed the technique on his own by transferring whatever he had learnt on khol and tabla to the *bani* or *bols* of the mardala. It was quite common those days, to have to rely more on one's capacity for assimilation and inborn talent than on any systematic training; both the disciplines of dance and music as well as several other artistic forms had suffered a severe jolt during the successive centuries of invasion and alien domination to which Orissa had been subjected to from the sixteenth century onward. And no traditional knowledge remained unaffected in the process. Whatever had survived was scattered and spurious in nature and demanded a high degree of imagination, talent and dedication to be carefully reassembled and carried forward.

Kelucharan was equally enterprising in the art of survival; when there was no job at the *panna baraja*, he would grow a beard and hair to escape notice and sell betel leaves on the streets of Puri. This attempt did not last long though, not only because the earning was almost nil but also because, despite the disguise, there would always be somebody who would recognize him and would start shouting: 'Krishna is selling *pan*! Krishna is selling *pan*!'

One day an old woman, whom he called Guruma, and who was like a second mother to him during his days in Mohansundar Goswami's troupe, recognized him on the road; she bought all the leaves from him and fed them to a cow which was passing by. She also gave him some extra money. After that day Kelucharan did not have the courage to continue selling *pan*.

Several months had passed since the day he left the Ras Leela party. Luck smiled on him one day when he was picked up to work in the *panna baraja* of a certain Loki Bhaina, who was a lover of music and an adept percussionist. He happened to hear Kelucharan sing while fetching buckets of water from the pool. At the end of the day, instead of the usual 20 *annas*, Loki Bhaina paid Kelucharan Rs. 100 and told him not to work any more as a labourer in the fields but to pursue his vocation in music. He asked Kelucharan to spend that money carefully and to return to him once the money was spent.

Few days later, Kelucharan's *Karna Mantra Guru*[1] told him that a certain Banamali Sahu, a zamindar suffering from leprosy, living at Khan Nagara, on the outskirts of Cuttack, was offering to pay Rs. 300 per month to anyone who would sing and play continuously the Nama Sankirtana at his house. Kelucharan went to Banamali Sahu and remained with him for a month and at the end of it the zamindar was so pleased with his devotional singing that instead of Rs. 300 gave him Rs. 1,001!

Cuttack, besides being the administrative capital of Orissa, was in those days also the main centre of cultural and educational activities. For the Mughals, the Marathas and the British, Cuttack had functioned as the administrative headquarters because of its easy accessibility provided by the two major rivers surrounding it: the

[1] In the Vaishnava tradition the *Karna Mantra Guru* is a sort of spiritual master who teaches the secret mantra or formula to the disciple by whispering it in his ears.

Mahanadi on the east and the Khatjouri on the west. During British rule a medical and an engineering school was set up at Jobra in Cuttack, the landing place for steamers coming from Calcutta. In the year 1870, thanks to the enlightened English Commissioner T.E. Ravenshaw, the first college, bearing his name, was founded in what came to be known as the Old College lane.

In 1903 the first literary organization of Orissa, the Utkal Sahitya Samaj, started its activities at Sri Ram Chandra Bhawan, near the Town Hall, the main objectives being to study and highlight the rich heritage of Oriya literature. As a branch of the Sahitya Samaj, the Utkal Sangeet Samaj was founded in the year 1933. Singhari Shyam Sundar Kar, a *vidwan* of Odissi music, taught there.

After a brief period of activity in Puri, Kalicharan Pattanayak, a leading figure in Oriya literature and performing arts, shifted his Ras Leela party to Cuttack, where later, in the year 1939, he founded the Orissa Theatres, bringing about a great revolution in the history of stage plays. One of his most successful plays, *Chakri* (1944), which was staged in those days at Banka Bazaar, left his audience spellbound. It was this play which Kelucharan, during his days in Banamali Sahu's residence, happened to see one evening.

Accustomed to the rudimentary lights and sets of Guru Goswami's Ras Leela stage presentations, the real theatre hall with curtains, sophisticated light effects and the high standard of rehersals by actors left him literally spellbound. After the show he could not move away and stood transfixed outside the theatre as if in a trance.

Durllav Chandra Singh, the director of the play, recognized him as the young Krishna of Mohansundar Goswami's troupe, having seen his performances whenever they were staged in Cuttack. In the past both he and Kalicharan Pattanayak had approached Mohan Goswami to let one of his boys perform temporarily in their plays. He now read in the boy's eyes a sense of amazed curiosity that had been produced by the play and asked him what he was doing at present. On hearing that he had left Mohansundar Goswami's party, he straight away proposed that Kelucharan work with them. Kelucharan readily accepted the offer; he just took a few days to go back to his village and give the money that he had earned to his mother and there he was, at the threshold of a new and exciting experience, full of expectations and eagerness to learn.

He was immediately hired for a small salary of Rs. 7 per month for doing a variety of jobs; from loading and unloading the stage sets and props to doing the make-up of the main artists, singing, playing the tabla and helping arrange the stage sets. In one of the plays, *Bonomala*, he even acted as the servant of Samuel Sahu (Babi) who did the role of the landlord. His role had a comic touch: he was seen cleaning a table while singing a love song addressed to it and fondly embracing it. The landlord would enter at this point and ask him what the hell he was doing and he would reply: 'Master, what else is there for me to embrace if not this table?', after which he would rush to the side wing and sit near Harihar Rout, the tabla teacher, and play the tabla for the rest of the play.

Kelucharan remained with the Orissa Theatres for a little less than a year. Although he learnt a lot during this period, he always had a feeling that his talent and potentialities were not being fully utilized. It so happened that one evening, during a performance, he could hardly play the tabla as he was suddenly seized with a bout of fever and had to lie down immediately. It turned out to be smallpox, *basanta*[2] as it is known in Orissa and it lasted for quite a few days. It seems Kalicharan Pattanayak did not show much concern towards Kelucharan during his illness; although he did visit him in the beginning and sent some homeopathic medicines, he paid him no attention afterwards. Moreover, when he left the stage due to the sudden fever, he had heard Kalicharan pass offensive remarks while enquiring about him. At that moment he decided that he would leave Orissa Theatres. This incident together with his realization that the Orissa Theatres was not offering him sufficient opportunities to exhibit his talent only strengthened his decision to leave.

He did not remain in his village for long; after a couple of days he was asked by a certain Buddhanath Routray to direct a Ras Leela party in Puri. At 21, for the first time Kelucharan took charge of a Ras party, known as the Radhakanta Ras Party and staged the performances in a *pandal* set up near the police station on the main road. The performances of *Mana Bhanjana* and *Balya Leela* drew large crowds and the earning was good. Kelucharan received Rs. 300 per month. The experiment was so successful that more than once Bauri Bandhu Mohanty, manager of the Annapurna A Theatre situated on the other side of the road,

[2] *Basanta* is an illness which has connection with Devi; the person affected by it is supposed to be visited by the Goddess and is venerated as one of her personifications during the course of the illness.

tried to discourage Kelucharan from continuing the Ras Leela performances and asked him to join them, since it was taking away the public from the theatre.

The Annapurna A Group in the early forties began training female dancers in an Oriental dance form popularly known as *Adhunika Geeta*, which was a mixture of adivasi and folk traditions, performed with light music. It had started to catch the imagination of the public due to its novelty and the presence of female dancers on stage (up until then male actors had played female roles). Although Kelucharan was attracted by all this, he was not fully convinced that it could be his cup of tea. His upbringing had been totally different; *bhakti* had always been the leitmotif in his art, and he was not sure how he would feel in a totally alien lifestyle.

After staging the two 'librettos' from Mohansundar Goswami's repertoire, Kelucharan set himself up as a director with the *nataka Meerabai*, in which he himself played the role of Rana Kumbha, Meerabai's husband.

Mahanta Maharaja, the head of the Emarmatha in Puri and one of the most powerful personalities of the Vaishnava community, liked the performance and asked Kelucharan to stage it in the *matha* during a festival. Fully immersed in the role of the dejected husband, Kelucharan, while calling out Meera's name fell on the ground and hit his chest. After the performance he ate too much of the food and pickles provided by the delighted Maharaja. The next day he was unable to get up. Members of his troupe wanted to hospitalize him, but he preferred to be left under the care of his brother in-law, in whose house he received massage and medicines. He was rather upset that the company did not pay him cash, with which he had planned to repay his relatives for the cost of the medicines, but paid him in kind by giving portions of food, rice, legumes and vegetables, which had been sent to the troupe by the Mahanta Maharaja after the performance and which he, still a convalescent, was unable to touch!

After spending a few days in his village, once again he caught a train to Puri with the intention of buying some more medicines and informing the Ras party that he needed some more days of rest before he could resume work. It so happened that on the same Bhubaneswar-Talcher passenger train the actor-director of the Orissa Theatres, Samuel Sahu (Babi) was also travelling, the man who had played the role of the landlord with Kelucharan as the servant. In that 15-minute journey, between Raghurajpur and Puri, Kelucharan came to know all that had happened after he had left the group a few months ago.

It was December 1945 and the War had just ended, when all the main actors decided to approach Kalicharan Pattanayak for a 25 per cent increase in their pay (which was around Rs. 8-10 per month) in view of the rising prices. But Pattanayak disagreed and proposed to increase only Babi's pay leaving the others with the old salary. Babi was the most senior and educated in the group. He had a diploma in engineering and had lost his job in the Chhotanagpur industries when it closed down in 1939 due to the War. When Kalicharan started the Orissa Theatres in 1940, Babi joined it as he had wanted to be an actor ever since he was a college student. Kalicharan's proposal in singling him out in giving a raise while ignoring the claims of others was totally unacceptable to him. As a result Babi along with the main actors including Priyanath Mishra, Madhu Polei, Bipin Pattanayak, Krishna Chandra Pande and others decided to leave the theatre. Only a few of the actors who played secondary roles remained behind, hoping that they would now have access to bigger roles.

The breakaway actors decided to form a new group and approached Somnath Das, the proprietor of the Annapurna Theatre Group (at that time called Annapurna Natya Mandali) for permission to use their premises in Cuttack which was only utilized by the group whenever in town. The building, situated on the Buxi Bazaar Road, belonged to a Marwari proprietor and was a cinema hall until the Annapurna Group took it on rent for staging their plays. In the space allotted to them a new company called Annapurna B Group was founded, which was to play a key role in the growth of the dance style later known as Odissi. The manager, a certain Lingaraj Nanda, from the village Khanduala Hota near the Chilka Lake, who had been associated with the Annapurna Natya Mandali since its inception, was quite enterprising and bold in his approach, always ready to experiment with new ideas and very fond of dance. It seems that in his childhood Lingaraj had learnt the *gotipua* dance in his native village. By this time the new group had already staged two plays, *Manager* and *Mulia* (the latter, written by Ramachandra Mishra, had a good run and was very well received) and now plans were a foot for staging the *nataka Devi*, for which they were still on the lookout for an artist who could play the lead female role. It was for this reason that Sahu Babi was going to Puri, to try and get some female artists from the A group.

Even before they reached Puri, Babi had already proposed to Kelucharan requesting him to join their group and the latter had enthusiastically accepted his proposal. The plan was that Babi would pick him up on his way back to Cuttack (even at this age Kelucharan did not venture to travel alone).

Once at Puri Kelucharan did not even go to see the Ras party. After buying the medicines, he returned immediately at the platform of the little station of Harikrishnapur, without any luggage, just wearing a torn dhoti with a *gamcha* slung on his shoulder and waited for Babi's arrival. By the time Babi was back it was 3 a.m.; it was pitch dark outside. Babi leaned out of the window to call him and Kelucharan appeared out of the dark managing to catch the train while it was still in motion. Life moved on towards a new destination and Kelucharan marched towards it without ever looking back, eagerly anticipating new opportunities to learn.

LOVE AT FIRST SIGHT

'ARE THESE the female artists you managed to bring along?', asked an annoyed Lingaraj Nanda on seeing Babi return from Puri with an unimpressive young lad instead of some attractive actresses. 'Keep him; he is a good tabla player', said Babi; and Kelucharan was kept on trial for the first month, during which he was to be given only food and lodging. From the second month he started receiving Rs. 15 a month.

Lingaraj Nanda had assembled a few boys and girls from the nearby villages and had entrusted the young Pankaj Charan Das, then in his late twenties, with the task of teaching them whatever at that point of time was known as 'dance', which meant moving the feet together and in rhythm, and miming a song. Pankaj Charan had learnt all this during the years spent at the Hajuri Theatre, a prominent repertory company (belonging to Balabhadra Hajuri Khuntia) at a hall located near the Lokanath Temple in Puri. The dance teacher over there was one Bhikari Charan Dolei.

Pankaj Charan Das in his early forties.

After the closing down of the Hajuri Theatre, young Pankaj, who had been exposed in his earlier years to the *mahari* dance performed in his aunt Ratnaprabha's house, started frequenting the *akhada jaga* located in each quarter of the town. At these centres, demonstrations and discussions on Odissi *sangeeta* and *vadya* along with selection of artists for the organization of the Sahi Jatra or ward festivals comprising sports, dance and music, were held. After spending a few years in the Pathara Akhada under the guidance of Jagu Mohanty he came to be associated with a number of drama troupes, prominent among them was the New Theatres of Orissa, operating in Baripada, the headquarter of the Mayurbhanj district, under the leadership of Radharamana Ray. Here he had the opportunity to learn and observe the vigorous Chhau dance style, and also to start teaching whatever dance training he had acquired until then.

Back in Puri he was associated for a little while with a Ras Leela party when a chance meeting with Lingaraj Nanda, always in search of new talent for his theatre, turned out to be one of the decisive moments in his life. He was at first asked to join the drama section, but as soon as his knowledge of dance became known, Lingaraj made him in-charge of training the few boys and girls that he had assembled. The short dance sequences composed by him served as sort of curtain raisers before the main play unfolded; for example, before the beginning of the play *Mulia*, a group of boys and girls would enter the stage in two lines and perform *desa vandana* (salutation to the Earth) by offering flowers and touching the earth. At the beginning of another play *Jaharo* (poison) while dancing they would shoot three arrows: after the first arrow the letter *ja* written on a small screen would be lowered from the top, after the second and third arrows the letters *ha* and *ro*, respectively. These dance interludes would last but a few minutes and would consist of very simple and stylized movements.

When Kelucharan joined the Annapurna B Group, he was asked to play the tabla while Pankaj was conducting the classes. It was not difficult for Kelucharan to pick up the six basic foot movements which were being taught and to guide the students in the absence of Pankaj. It was at this juncture that his aptitude for dance became known.

In the meantime, while the play *Benami* was presented (at the beginning of which Pankaj was engaged in a comic role along with the female dancer, Uma Sossi), the rehearsals for the *nataka Devi*, written by Ramachandra Mishra and to be directed by Samuel Sahu (Babi), had begun. There was scope for a short dance composition at the beginning of the *nataka*. The selected piece was based on the mythological story of the victory of Mohini over the demon Bhasmasura, and had three main characters, one female and two males. The female dancer for the part of Mohini had not yet been chosen; Pankaj Charan assigned the role of

Mahadeva to Kelucharan and kept that of Bhasmasura for himself. This at first was supposed to be danced in the Chhau style by Radha Krishna Bhanja from Baripada. On this occasion Lingaraj Nanda himself went to Puri and brought back (from the A Group) the star dancer Laxmipriya who had been associated with the Annapurna Theatre almost since its inception. She was immediately selected for the role of the temptress Mohini and in about seven days, the fifteen-minute dance-drama was ready to be shown for the manager's approval.

On stage the backdrop depicted the Mount Kailasha, the abode of Shiva, and the jungle where the *asura* was engaged in deep meditation. Pleased by his devotion Mahadeva appears before him and while dancing tells him that he is the creator, preserver and destroyer of all beings and could grant him any boon. The demon asks for the power to convert into ashes whomsoever he touches with his hands. The request is immediately granted and the demon, eager to try his new power, rushes towards Mahadeva, who in desperation calls Narayana for help. Narayana appears disguised as a charming woman, Mohini and the *asura*, totally captivated by her beauty, asks her to become his wife. She challenges him to win her over in a dance competition; the *asura* accepts the challenge and though ignorant about dance, he merely imitates what Mohini does until he places his hand over his own head and thereby turns into ashes. At this point Mahadeva reappears and enchanted by Mohini's beauty, attempts to embrace her, only to find instead a laughing Narayana who tries to cheer up a shame-faced Mahadeva by telling him that all this is happening by virtue of his creation of *maya* (illusion).

Both the dance sequences, the one based on a *tala* of 10 *matras* danced by Mahadeva and the one performed by Mohini in 16 *matras* were composed by Pankaj Charan, and although they could not be said to be in the Odissi style yet, they certainly created history. Everybody in the troupe was astonished to see their *genda mundia* (or 'bald head' as Kelucharan was affectionately called by his elders) dancing so well. Samuel Sahu (Babi), his *dada*, had known Kelucharan as the comic servant in the play where he was the landlord and had brought him as a good tabla player. And the other director in the troupe, Priyanath Mishra, would not allow anybody else to do his make-up except Kelu, but nobody had ever imagined that this lad, in addition to all that, could also dance! Babi called him aside and told him: 'Kelu, forget about acting, it is not for you (it seems Kelucharan was stammering at this stage and got rid of it later by repeating the *pakhawaji bols* in a fast tempo). You must pursue a career in dance.'

After the success of this venture, Lingaraj Nanda got a *gotipua* master named Krishna Chandra Mohapatra who taught Laxmipriya to render two Oriya songs through dance, '*Janare mo rana parama mita*' (my dear friend, this is my promise) and '*Nahi ki karidela*' (the one who denied). Both the lyrics were by Kishor Kavi Shyam Sundar Das and set to music by Balakrishna Das and the lyricist himself, respectively.

This was in the year 1946; little did Lingaraj Nanda know at this point that his idea of getting a *gotipua* master to teach his female dancer would be instrumental in bringing about a revolution one day!

Kelucharan did not have the courage to reveal his past experience as a *gotipua* dancer to Krishna Chandra (and for that matter to anybody in the troupe, perhaps still troubled by his father's utter contempt towards this dance form) and he just accompanied the two *abhinaya* pieces on the pakhawaj. But Krishna Chandra did not stay for long, and after his departure, it was Kelucharan who conducted the rehearsals of the two songs with Laxmipriya and even added a short sequence of *vadya pallavi* or rhythmic dance based on the *ektali teka* (4 beats) '*dindha tennaka dhinni ta*'.

Laxmipriya got an opportunity to present the second of the two songs in the next play *Abhisek*, written by Aswini Kumar Ghosh; the script centred around the coronation of Kapilendra Dev, the king of Puri, and the dance was performed before the play started. The accompaniment on mardala was provided by Kelucharan and the songs were rendered by Haribabu accompanied by a harmonium. Laxmipriya wore the sari in the *dakhini* (south Indian) style, with one end folded in between the legs and tucked in at the waist from behind and the other end pinned on to the blouse and let loose at the back.

The effect on the audience was stunning; people had never imagined the existence of such a graceful dance and that it could be presented on the stage. With the female temple dancers almost extinct by now, the only dance that people could watch, was the one performed by the young boys (the *gotipua*) inside the *mathas* during religious functions or open air Jatra performances and public festivals. Laxmipriya was undoubtedly a beautiful young woman endowed with a supple body and expressive liquid eyes; she had been groomed in the theatre atmosphere (A Group) since she was seven and had learnt folk and tribal dances that were being taught there.

The dance masters in the A Group, who also functioned as directors and actors depending on the requirement, were Kashinath Sahu from Pipli, Laxminarayan Patra from Gudiali in Ganjam and Kartik Kumar Ghosh, brother of the playwright Aswini Kumar Ghosh, from Cuttack. Each of them had received a mixed type of training in dance.

The first master had received some training in the *akhada nrutya* from Ramachandra Mania, an Odissi *sangeeta* exponent from Jatni in Puri district, and in *abhinaya* from Bolei Banerjee during his association with the Radha Krishna Theatre, the first professional theatre to be founded in 1918, with its headquarter in Cuttack. The second had been trained in the folk theatre tradition of the Prahalad Nataka, a performing art form of the Ganjam area, which involved

Laxmipriya (extreme right) performing Adivasi dance during the Republic Day celebrations in Delhi in the early 1950s.

music, vigorous dance and acting. And the third master had attended a six-month summer course in Almora, where Uday Shankar, the doyen of the revival of the Indian dance tradition, had opened a centre in 1940 for imparting training in various dance styles. All these influences went into the formation of the first of the group dances which the young girls associated with the A Group performed on stage, usually at the beginning of the play.

The first batch of girls had been associated with the A Group since the early forties; while most of them were from Puri, others had been brought in by the male dancers in the group from their respective villages. Laxmipriya, although born in Khurda, had at a very early age come to live in Puri with her mother Tulsi Devi. She was the youngest among the first batch of dancers, along with Heera, daughter of a *devadasi* of Puri, and Nirmala, who had left behind the rest of her family in Calcutta, and, at the age of seven, had settled down in Puri with her mother. Among the other dancers who were already married at the time of joining the theatre were Radharani, Haramani, Balamani, Sara, Ratna and Buddhi. Some of them had had stage experience having participated either in folk dramas in their respective villages or having been cast by Mohansundar Dev Goswami in his film *Sita Bibaha*. After joining the theatre, they were left completely under the care of the manager Bauri Bandhu Mohanty, who would treat all of them like his own daughters. Slowly, besides dancing, they started to replace the male actors in female roles and grow as full-fledged artists.

In the first ten years of its existence, the A Group did not have a permanent stage to perform and used to set up camps in various districts of the state for a full season or performed in make-shift *pandals*. During the rainy season, the entire troupe would stay in the rented hall in Cuttack to rehearse new plays. Only after the B Group occupied this space, the A Group settled down permanently in Puri in a three-storeyed building located on the Bada Danda, in front of the police station. Although the compound had been given on a five-year lease contract by the Mahant of Uttara Parswa Math, it became the permanent base of the A Group and after the construction of the stage, it came to be known as the Annapurna A Theatre.

By the time Lingaraj Nanda went to fetch Laxmipriya for the B Group, she was almost seventeen and had acted

Folk dancers gather in Delhi to celebrate the Republic Day. Laxmipriya (left) is seen here with Indira Gandhi (centre), and Lingaraj Nanda (extreme right).

as Madhavi, the main heroine, in the drama 'PWD' (Public Works Department) and appeared in a few solo dances, besides some group dances. One of the group dances performed by Laxmipriya, Sara and Haramani, had been composed by Kashinath Sahu in a style akin to the Manipuri, set to an Oriya song '*Manara kotha kohibi kahara sakhi re*' (to whom shall I tell the secrets of my heart, oh friend?). As a solo number, she would perform the dance for the song '*Nila Jamuna kule Kalia*' (Krishna on the bank of the dark Jamuna) composed in folk style by Laxminarayan Patra.

Her stage presence and aptitude for dance which had already been evident on the A Group platform, came to the notice of the public with her dance performance for the B Group; she literally mesmerized the audience and earned immense admiration for herself and the dance she performed. It was her performance which in the following years was to inspire the first batch of girls to learn Odissi dance despite the social ostracism.

Within a span of a few months, in the year 1946, the three main professional theatre groups, that is the Annapurna A and B Groups, and the Orissa Theatres of Kalicharan

Pattanayak, seemed to compete with each other in presenting a sample of the Odissi dance on stage by a female dancer, although till then the appellative Odissi still referred more to the music than to a distinctive style of dance. In July of the same year, Kalicharan Pattanayak staged his own play *Abhijan*, directed by Adwaita Charan Mohanty and Durllav Chandra Singh, which included a dance by Sara, a female dancer, presenting within the context of the drama, a *mahari* song at the court of King Purushuttam Dev.

Almost simultaneously, the A Group, presented the play *Kavisurja*, based on the life and work of the Oriya poet Kavisurya Baladeva Ratha, where a female dancer, Haramani, performed a short sequence of Odissi *bols* at the court of the raja of Athaghara. Written by Ramachandra Mishra, the play was directed by Kartik Kumar Ghosh. The *gotipua* master Harihara Panda taught the dance sequence to Haramani Devi.

Although it is difficult to establish if the dance number presented by Laxmipriya in the play *Abhisek* preceeded or followed the other two, one can safely assign her the credit of having been not only among the first female dancers to present solo public performances in Odissi style on stage, but above all to have inspired a host of young girls to learn the dance in the years to come. The dances for these two songs were rendered by Laxmipriya, and later on by other female dancers of the troupe, either as solo dance pieces or as part of court scenes woven into the dramatic plots. This also gave Kelucharan and Laxmipriya the opportunity to work in close association either as dancers or as one accompanying the other on the pakhawaj.

After her personal success in the play *Abhisek*, Laxmipriya was cast as the main heroine in the next *nataka Feriah* (The Return), a socio-political play written by Gopal Chhotray and directed by Samuel Sahu (Babi). Appealing to strong patriotic feelings, the play took its inspiration from Mahatma Gandhi's appeal to the youngsters, on the eve of India's Independence, to return to their native villages and work among the masses. The play, premiered on 9 August 1946 ran full house until December of the same year, and turned out to be one of the most successful presentations of the B Group.

Sadhava Jhia (The Merchant's Daughter), written by Adwaita Charan Mohanty was the next play to be staged and the directors of the B Group assembled along with the writer to discuss the plot. Lingaraj Nanda was keen on having a dance sequence in the play, and the right situation had to be devised. The story was about the legendary Tapoi and her seven brothers, who leave her behind with their wives to sail across the seas to the distant islands of Java and Sumatra to sell their merchandise. It was decided that the Oriya merchants would perform a mythological dance in order to attract the Balinese people and exhibit their products (among the goods to be sold were *pata chitra* representing gods and goddesses of the Hindu pantheon). Durllav Chandra Singh, the director of the play, suggested that a dance sequence based on the *Dashavatara* (the ten incarnations of Lord Vishnu), a poem from Jayadeva's *Gita Govinda* be composed for the purpose. This lyrical poem was sung by him in his role as Jayadeva in the *Jayadeva Nataka* staged in 1943 by Kalicharan Pattanayak. A decision was taken to retain the *tala* of 10 beats and the raga Shuddh Kalyan as in the earlier composition of the dance.

What emerged was a result of the combined effort of more than one person; each individual contributing in his capacity to make what was later to be labelled as a historic event in the evolution of Odissi dance. It is difficult to determine the exact contribution of each individual. One can only attempt to recreate the scene, capture the charged atmosphere and let the tale flow by itself. Durllav Chandra with his experience not only contributed as the director of the play but also as mridanga and tabla player, singer and actor; Pankaj Charan as dance master, Kelucharan as dancer and tabla player; Hariharan Rout and Madhu Polei as tabla player and music master respectively; Lingaraj Nanda and Adwaita Charan Mohanty as coordinators and advisers.

Durllav Chandra was the last among the artistes to leave Kalicharan Pattanayak's Theatre Group; he had been with the master for 19 years from the age of 11 and was like a son to him. He had been part of the Ras Leela troupe directed by Kalicharan for the first eight years, first in Puri and then in Cuttack. Later, when the Orissa Theatres were formed he became fully involved with all its activities. Kalicharan appreciated his willingness to learn through listening and observation. In Kalicharan's house in Cuttack there would always be a gathering of musicians, poets, dramatists, and discussions and demonstrations of dance and music and exchange of ideas took place.

The young Durllav endowed with a sharp memory would

not miss a chance to listen and absorb all that he was exposed to; melodies, rhythms, poetry, dance steps were all avidly imbibed and recreated by his fertile imagination. He learnt to play the khol during the evening *arati* which was a regular feature in Kalicharan's house; the progression from the khol to the tabla and dhrupad pakhawaj had been smooth. Hariharan Rout, the other tabla player in the troupe, had learnt from him. He had picked up the theoretical know-ledge of the *shastric* aspects of the arts from Kalicharan, while his expertise in dance was derived more from observa-tion than from *riyaz*. What prevented him from practicing dance were the attacks of rheumatic fever which would often leave his joints weak. It was after one of these attacks that finally, at the age of 29, he and his wife, Laxmipriya an actress and dancer from the same group, decided to leave Kalicharan and join the others who had formed the B Group.

In the dance piece *Dashavatara,* Durllav's contribution has been crucial as far as the rhythmic score is concerned; the *bols* (rhythmic syllables) that were set for the dance in 1947 have remained more or less the same and are still used by the present Odissi dancers, the only difference being that earlier they were played by Durllav in the *dhrupad* style, and now they have been changed into the Odissi *bani* by Kelucharan. For example, the initial sequence sounded as follows:

> *dha tette dage kruda tette, ta tette tage kruda tette, dheredhere kititaka dhei dhei taka, dhuma kita dhum kita taka, taka dhum dhum kita taka. . . .*

And later on became:

> *ta itti nakadataka dhina kette, ta itti nakadataka dhinna kette, dheitere ketetaka dhei dhei ta, tatin nam ta tatin nam, tatin nam ta tatin nam. . . .*

And the sequence of syllables after the Buddha *avatar* was:

> *kdan dhumakete dhdan taktak dhumakita, dhdan dhumakita takdhuma kitatak dhumakita. . . .*

This later became:

> *tam dadhigene dhei tam dadhigene, dhei tingine dheitin ginedhei tingine.*

Specific *mudra* or hand gestures were required to distinguish one *avatar* from the other, and the people involved in the composition of dance were not yet acquainted with texts, *Natya Shastra* or *Abhinaya Darpana*. For information on the subject, Durllav suggested that the book, *Dances of India,* by Projesh Bannerjee, containing descriptions and drawings of the different *mudras*, should be consulted. Dr A.C. Mohanty helped in procuring the book from Calcutta, and for the first time in Orissa a dance sequence was composed following the guidelines of a written text as far as hand gestures were concerned.

The rhythmic score was set by Durllav Chandra (who also helped in the selection of correct *mudras*), Hariharan Rout and Kelucharan. Pankaj Babu choreographed the dance sequences. He was assisted by Lingaraj Nanda and Adwaita Charan Mohanty in understanding the Sanskrit *slokas.* Kelucharan and Laxmipriya were the two dancers, the former playing the lead role; not only was Kelucharan translating into action Pankaj Charan's and Durllav's instructions but also teaching them to Laxmipriya and embellishing them with his own insight and sensibility.

This dance composition has remained more or less unchanged even till today. In an alternating sequence of *abhinaya* portions the ten *avatars* are introduced through hand gestures and facial expressions, and rhythmic interludes with appropriate dance steps to suit the character of each *avatar* were performed in between. While the pure dance sequences were executed by the dancers together, in the *abhinaya* portions it was Kelucharan who presented the interpretation of the song, with Laxmipriya standing with *anjali hasta* (joined hands) as a *bhakta* (devotee).

For this dance Laxmipriya wore a velvet blouse or *kanchala* over which a chaddar was draped in the shape of a '*v*' at the back and falling in two bands on the chest; Kelucharan's dhoti and Laxmipriya's sari were both worn in the *pheri kacchi* style of the *gotipua*, with their end portions tucked in the back. Both dancers wore a *moti mala* (bead necklace) and a *mukuta* as headgear.

The success of this performance opened up prospects for the Odissi dance style, but at the same time it revealed its limitations in training and that it lacked a firm and systematic foundation. It was at this point that the fortuitous arrival of Dayal Sharana's troupe in Cuttack from Andhra Pradesh proved to be a crucial event for both the

Kelucharan and Laxmipriya performing the Dashavatara *(facing page).*

history of dance in Orissa as well as for Kelucharan's growth as a dancer.

A Telugu by birth, Dayal Sharana had been trained in a number of Indian dance styles, such as the Kathak from the north and the Bharatanatyam from the south, before joining the India Cultural Centre at Almora, founded in the early forties by Uday Shankar, a pioneer in the revival of Indian dance traditions. Here Dayal was exposed not only to the teaching of the other two dance styles, i.e. the Manipuri from the north-east and the Kathakali from the south, but above all to the eclectic and creative approach in dance training which was characteristic of Uday Shankar's method of teaching. Unfortunately, he had to leave the centre even before its closure in 1944, due to an attack of tuberculosis. After recovery Dayal founded his own school of dance in Visakhapatnam. He used to tour other states with his group of dancers, giving performances in rented theatres in towns and selling tickets for the shows.

On one such trip Dayal had come to Cuttack along with six or seven of his dancers for presenting his work and had rented the Annapurna Theatre hall for three evening performances. The sale of tickets for the first two evenings had not at all been encouraging and he feared that he would be unable to pay even the rent of the hall. He had in the meantime watched the dance rehearsals of Kelucharan and Laxmipriya and was so impressed by what he saw that he proposed to Lingaraj Nanda to have a joint programme of both the troupes on the third evening. The Annapurna troupe opened its dance performance with the *Dashavatara*, followed by '*Nahi ki koridela*' and the *Mohini Bhasmasura* dance-sequence; the Dayal troupe performed their dance items after the interval among which were two solos by him: the *Hunter* and the *Surya*. The Oriya public, represented in larger numbers than on the first two evenings, expressed its appreciation for the indigenous dance sequences—clapping more vigorously during the first half of the programme than on the second. In spite of the good turnout of people, Dayal failed to raise enough money for the rent of the hall.

He then proposed to Lingaraj Nanda that he be allowed to pay back his debt by directing a dance production for the Annapurna Theatre. He had already set his eyes on Kelucharan and was looking forward to an opportunity to teach this promising lad everything he knew. Lingaraj accepted the proposal but suggested that he teach his style to Pankaj Charan instead of Kelucharan. The new dance composition was to be performed at the beginning of the play *Radhika*, written by Adwaita Charan Mohanty and directed by Durllav Chandra Singh.

Durllav Chandra was also very keen that Kelucharan should be exposed to Dayal's dance style; he specially admired the variety of styles Dayal knew and was particularly impressed by the neat presentation of the group choreographies which revealed a much more sophisticated approach in comparison to the Annapurna Theatre's output. The group dances of the B Group till then had been more of stylization of steps and arm movements performed in unison than real choreographies. He was very keen that Dayal should teach Kelucharan the art of composition and whatever one needs to know to be able to create new dance sequences. However Dayal started, as per Lingaraja's wishes, to work with Pankaj Charan; but it did not last long, since it seems that after a few sessions Pankaj admitted defeat. He called Kelucharan and told him: '*Kelu, tu sikha! Mora onta bhanga heu ni*' (Kelu, you learn! My body is too stiff).

With this training Kelucharan embarked upon one of the most intense and exciting experience of his apprenticeship. An experience that prepared him to take off, confident and aware that he possessed the power and the creativity to compose a dance on any subject. Guru Kelucharan was born out of this encounter; and it is significant that it should be the Uday Shankar touch, although transmitted through one of his students, which lit one more spark of creativity in the world of dance. And not an ordinary one for that matter!

In Kelucharan's words:

Dayal Sharana showed me the way; he made me conscious of what my body was doing and what more could be achieved through exercises. He made me aware of the use of the different *mudra* of the hands and of the possibilities of utilizing the same hand gestures for expressing different actions (*viniyoga*). Not that I was not using *mudra* before, but I was not aware of it. He explained to me the derivation of the various hand gestures starting from the actions of everyday life: he would ask me to observe my hands while I was drinking water or eating food or holding an object and from there he would go to the *shastric* name of the *mudra*. He made me understand that although there are classified *mudras* in the written texts, many more could be created deriving them from the observation of everyday life. He taught me how to compose small sequences of dance by putting together different steps; he opened in front of me the door of 'creativity' and once I went beyond its threshold I never looked back.

Kelucharan was an avid and attentive pupil; none else in the group had the patience and devotion to learn as he did. He would get up before dawn to perform the body exercises taught to him until he could master them, careful not to miss a single chance to learn more. He would send money home to get *gua ghia* (ghee made from pure cow milk) with which he massaged his facial muscles in order to render them supple and ready to reproduce the difficult movements shown by Dayal; each part of the face was exercised separately and had to reproduce contrasting emotions. He learnt how to cry with one half of the face and laugh with the other half; how to move the eyebrows alternately and how to express an entire range of sentiments with the use of the eyes alone. The versatility and fluidity of expressions in rendering *abhinaya*, for which he became famous later on, can be partly attributed to the intense facial training he received during this period. The training was also the source of the exceptionally supple and sinuous movements of his back and arms which continued to distinguish his dance even at a later stage.

This was the first and only contact, although indirect, that Kelucharan had with Uday Shankar's training and through it with other dance styles. In the early fifties when Shankar's film *Kalpana* (Immagination) was shown for months together at the Prabhat Cinema Hall in Cuttack, Kelucharan watched it no less than forty times! These two giants met only once, much later, in the early seventies when after a show of *Shankarscope*[1] in Delhi, Kelucharan went backstage accompanied by one of his students interested in interviewing Shankar who was quite old by then and was not dancing any more. For Kelucharan it was an emotional encounter nevertheless. Years ago, in the mid fifties, Uday Shankar was to be the chief guest at a function in Calcutta where one of Kelucharan's student, Minakshi Nanda, was presenting the *Shiva Nataraja* dance, reworked on the pattern of the one performed by him earlier in the *Mohini Bhasmasura* dance-drama. But due to a sudden strike which paralyzed the city, the chief guest could not reach the venue on time and the meeting between the two great artists never took place.

After completing the group dance on Radha and Krishna

[1]A type of variety show which combined stage and screen together with magical effects. It was produced and directed by Uday Shankar in the late sixties and had a run of about 100 shows.

for the Annapurna Group, for the next two years Dayal Sharana kept in touch with them by returning to Cuttack at regular intervals. During each visit he taught something valuable to his earnest student; Kelucharan on his part continued practising the different body exercises even during Dayal's absence, improving and refining his dance movements more and more. As a result, Lingaraj Nanda did not hesitate in entrusting Kelucharan with the direction of the dance sequence to be included in the next play *Aloka*, produced by Priyanath Mishra; the piece, performed by Laxmipriya in three different styles, Manipuri, Odissi and Kathak, was the first dance piece to be fully composed by Kelucharan. The style was derived from the one taught by Dayal Sharana; which included a variety of traditions; as usual Kelucharan accompanied the dance on tabla and pakhawaj.

It was during this new venture that the friendship and affection between Kelucharan and Laxmipriya developed. And after years of intense collaboration, it finally blossomed into a full-fledged relationship. Kelucharan had admired her beauty and talent since he first saw her dancing in group dances on the stage of the A Group. Laxmipriya had started training both in dance and acting from the age of seven, when along with her mother, she had been chosen to join the troupe by Bauri Bandhu Mohanty, the manager of the A Group. Since then she had been treated like a daughter by him, and both of them had been provided living quarters within the theatre premises. That was around the year 1938 when the Annapurna Group had started functioning and had been in existence for a couple of years. Since the day Laxmipriya had been brought to Cuttack by Lingaraj Nanda to join the B Group, Kelucharan had been by her side, as a dance partner as well as a trusted friend. She found in him the sense of security which she had been deprived of since childhood, having been brought up without a proper family. He was somebody whom she could instinctively trust, particularly because of the devotion and sincerity which he displayed towards his work.

For Kelucharan it was a question of total commitment; Laxmipriya was, and continues to be even after 50 years, his 'inspiration'. She possessed everything which he was looking for: she was beautiful, had an excellent sense of rhythm, good musical sense, grace, talent and trusted him completely.

Kelucharan and Laxmipriya, soon after marriage, in the late 1940s.

Although extremely fond of her since the very beginning, Kelucharan did not take the initiative in declaring his love for her; a refusal on the part of the girl would have meant loss of credibility and prestige. It was Laxmipriya who made the first move, and she did it in the most romantic manner: by sending a red *gulabi fullo* (red rose) to his changing room at the end of a rehearsal. From then on their relationship became more intense, but nobody knew about it for quite some time.

Their union took place secretly, on the stage, sanctified by the *prasada* (sacred food) brought from the Chandi Mandir in Cuttack. It was a simple ceremony which included an exchange of garlands, the application of *sindoor* (vermilion) on her forehead and the promise made by him to her mother that he would take care of her daughter all his life. The stage was where they met and got united; the ceremony in the temple of Lokanath in Puri took place a couple of years later, in order to make that promise still more binding and *indissolubile*. And for Kelucharan that promise is just as sacred even today. He needs her by his side whenever engaged in a new composition; even now she is the 'inspiration' from where and for whom his creativity flows.

Lingaraj Nanda was not very happy on discovering the engagement; he immediately foresaw that sooner or later the two of them would leave the group and be on their own. Strangely enough even Laxmipriya's mother never accepted willingly her daughter's decision; she was a very impulsive woman and although she had been an actress in her younger days, of late she had become a *mataji* observing strictly all the austere rules of the Vaishnava sect. Although the mother stayed with them, she did not eat the food cooked in their kitchen; instead she would cook on her own. Maybe she had in mind a match from a higher caste and different profession for her daughter's hand; unfortunately she died a couple of years later and did not live long enough to see Kelucharan's rise in life.

When Laxmipriya became pregnant some months later, Lingaraj Nanda thought it would be better for Kelucharan to go away for some time (maybe he was still hopeful to be able to separate them) and, hence, sent him to Raghurajpur for few months. By the time he returned, Laxmipriya, not in a position to dance any more, proceeded to Puri along with her mother to stay at the Annapurna A Theatre premises. Charu, the first daughter, was born while Kelucharan was away in Sambalpur on a tour giving performances; by the time he received the telegram about the birth of his daughter, Laxmipriya had already resumed dancing. In fact, she had her first dance programme within 21 days of the delivery. The programme took place in Puri on the occasion of the visit by the Governor; Bonomali Maharana, Kelucharan's first cousin, played the mardala for her on this occasion.

After Laxmipriya's return to the B Group, along with mother and daughter, Kelucharan was given charge of the dance composition for the next drama, *Nara Devata*, to be directed by Durllav Chandra Singh. The two solo dance pieces in the play, one in the *raj durbar* and the other by Urvashi to entice Arjuna doing penance, were performed by Hemalata and Durllav's wife also named Laxmipriya, respectively. The latter learned to perform the dance for the Odissi song, '*Nahi ki koridela*' from Kelucharan; she still remembers how, although a mother of two at that time, she once burst into tears in the greenroom after receiving a slap from Kelucharan for having made a mistake. In this

Charu, Kelucharan's first daughter, dancing at the age of six.

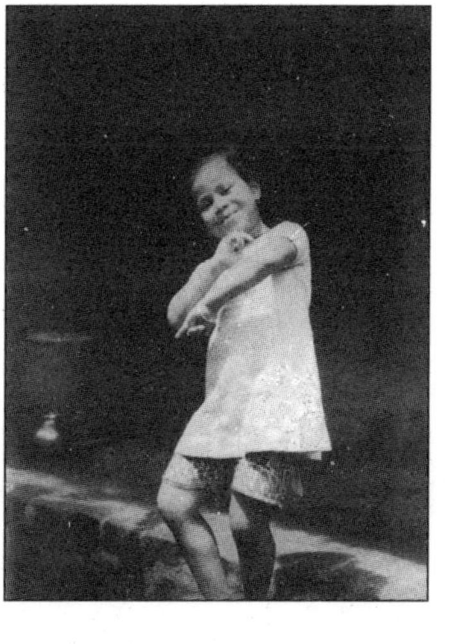

Kelucharan in the late 1950s.

play Kelucharan did the comic role of an effeminate dance teacher who with his students (Laxmipriya, Monimala, Hemalata and others) performs a group dance in the *raj durbar.*

Somehow the relations between Lingaraj Nanda and the duo Kelucharan-Laxmipriya were rather strained. He realized that they would not remain with him for long and started drifting away from them. Laxmipriya was the first to leave and returned to Puri along with her mother and daughter, while Kelucharan continued teaching dance compositions to other female dancers, preparing the ground for his departure. A few months later, while he was busy loading the truck after a performance at Pipli, Kelucharan received a telegram from Laxmipriya informing him of her mother's death.

The same night Kelucharan left the B Group and after a three-day journey he met Laxmipriya at Keonjhar where she and her daughter were stationed along with other members of the Annapurna A Group. Together the three of them returned to Puri and it was only then that their union received the blessing of Lokanath as a further promise of perpetual partnership. On the way back from the Lokanath Temple Laxmipriya bought an image of a smiling Shiva from a roadside seller at Bada Danda; this was the first sacred image to be installed in the puja room when they settled down in their own house in Cuttack about ten years later. For many years, before the *murti* of Jagannath was given the central place in the small temple in their house, the image of Shiva had been the driving force behind Kelucharan's determined struggle. His first dance was dedicated to Shiva and He remains his favourite God.

During their five to six months stay in Puri Kelucharan directed the dance sequence to the *Upendra Bhanja Nataka* staged by the Annapurna A Group. The famous eighteenth century Oriya poet Upendra Bhanja, deeply distressed by the death of his wife due to a snake bite, had become a vagabond and during his wanderings composed the Oriya poem *Baidehisa Bilasa* (based on the *Ramayana* story) sitting in front of a Kali temple. It is said that while he was singing it, Lavanyavati, a *devadasi*, appeared in front of Upendra Bhanja and performed a dance. To interpret this role, Laxmipriya learnt some dance steps from Asha Devi, an old *mahari* of the Puri Temple and showed them to Kelucharan. We can probably consider the four sequences of dance composed by him for this occasion as the basic structure of what later on became the traditional opening item of an Odissi dance recital. This introductory piece, which was later known as *mangala charan*, included the *puspanjali* (offering of flowers), *bhumi pranam* (salutation to the Earth), the two sets of *bols*: *tari kita dhi* (from the *gotipua* repertoire of Agadhu Maharana) and *thei thei* (composed by Kelucharan for the group dance in *Nara Devata*), followed by the triple salutations: over the head, in front of the face and in front of the chest.[2]

Inspired by Lavanyavati's dance, in which he saw his wife Kolavati, Upendra Bhanja composed the famous song '*Kanto bina diba rajani sajani*' (without my husband, days and nights appear very long, oh friend). In her role as a *devadasi* Laxmipriya interpreted this song in her dance. It concluded with a brief sequence of pure dance. In composing these dances Kelucharan drew inspiration from both the *gotipua* and *mahari* styles. He included some of the *bhauri* or *chakramandali* (circular movements) which the *mahari* used to perform during their dance at the time of *arati* held after Lord Jagannath's morning meal in the temple.

The music for the dance pieces was composed by Hari Panda. The costume worn by Laxmipriya was in the typical *mahari* style: the velvet *kanchala* on top, the chaddar tied around the waist and the sari draped from the waist downward.

The day the production was to be staged, both Kelucharan and Laxmipriya ate non-vegetarian food against the advice of Asha Devi. Soon after the *mangala charan* was over Laxmipriya threw up in the green room. She tried to continue with the *abhinaya* piece but she was only half way through when she had an attack of diarrhoea and fainted on the stage. The show had to be suspended. It was resumed three days later when Laxmipriya had recovered. From that day, for many years, Kelucharan never yielded again to the temptation to eat meat on the days he had to dance on stage.

[2] In a text written in the eighteenth century by Lavanya Mahari, *Devadasi nrutya karika* the triple salutation at the end of the dance is described as follows: '*Aparena mandire tatra tridha pranamama chareta, anjalikara sanmyoge tridhabhinandane chareta sarbadou hrudaye tatra duitiye siramandala natanga bibhupadecha mangalanu-chareta sadha*' (Another in the temple salutes thrice with folded palms. First of all at the heart, secondly at the head then near the feet of the Lord while performing the *mangala charan*).

ODISSI DANCE: AN OBSESSION FOR LIFE

SINCE 1949 Kelucharan had started giving private dance tuitions in Cuttack. Although dance had not yet become part of the general education of an average Oriya girl and was still considered disreputable by the middle- and higher-class of the society, some parents had the courage to defy social conventions and provide dance training to their daughters.

Laxmipriya's dance had fascinated more than one girl. Small Minati (later to become Mishra) still remembers how she would run from her house, situated in front of the Annapurna Theatre in Cuttack, just in time to watch Laxmipriya dance *'Nahi ki koridela'* and get back before her parents noticed her absence. Sanjukta's mother never missed any of the dance presentations at the Annapurna Theatre and did not hesitate to ask Kelucharan to teach her five-year old daughter the first steps of that dance. Sanjukta's father, Abhiram Mishra, a Brahmin by caste and an electrical engineer by profession, although not very happy about it to start with, later on had to yield to the fierce determination of both wife and daughter and allowed the latter to go to Madras to learn the rigorous Bharatanatyam style from Rukmini Devi Arundale.

Kumkum Das's mother belonged to a zamindar family in Jajpur in Orissa; she had often witnessed performances by itinerant groups of artists who would come and perform in the courtyard of her parents' house. These performing groups included the *gotipua* from Puri district, the Danda

Nacha[1] from south Orissa, and folk dancers from the western part of Orissa; although allowed to watch the shows from behind a purdah, she did not miss a single performance and would often dream of being able to learn those captivating songs and dances. After her early marriage to a mathematician, she came to Cuttack and saw Laxmipriya's dance at the Annapurna Theatre; her first daughter Bandana (nicknamed Mira) was one of the first students to receive training from Kelubabu in their own house, while her younger daughter Kumkum started training a few years later.

Satish Chandra Ghosh, Jayanti's father, a Bengali educationist settled in Cuttack, was the driving force behind his third daughter's dance training: unaffected by the dire warnings of his colleagues that his daughter would not be able to find a husband if allowed to continue dancing, he would dismiss them by saying: 'For the time being let her dance, we will think about her marriage when the time comes'.

Minakshi Nanda belonged to a musically inclined Brahmin family; her father, a secretary in the law department during the British raj, was an amateur sitar player while her elder brother had learnt tabla for some years from Pundit Jnan Prakash and her elder sister was a light-music singer. Little Minakshi's aptitude for dance was discovered quite early; since the tender age of three she was able to present the folk dance steps learnt effortlessly from her middle sister. When Kelucharan was called in to teach her she was only four years old and at five she was already giving her first public performance: a little doll dressed up as mini Shiva with a tiger skin around the loins, strings of beads on her bare chest and the crest of the moon sitting on her head.

When Kunkumina's father invited Kelucharan home to teach his eldest daughter, she was only two and a half years old. After class, Kelucharan would take her for a ride on his cycle. A year later, in 1955, she gave a performance at the Kumar Utsava Samiti; she was accompanied on to the dais and introduced to the audience by the music and dance director Surendra Mohanty. Her dress for that occasion, stitched by Krishna Chandra Rath, was in red satin, with a golden *zari* border all along the edge to form the *kumbha* design, while the ornaments were of paper-board covered with silver paper. Kelucharan had done elaborate drawings

[1]So called because the main characters hold a *danda* or stick while dancing. It is a sort of ritualistic dance-drama performed in the villages of coastal and central Orissa during the last 14 days preceeding the advent of the new Oriya year (*Pana Sankranti* which falls around the middle of April).

on her forehead and along her cheeks. Her dance debut, although only 5 minute long, was a great success.

Sadhana's father, Shri Raj Gobinda Bose a police officer and her mother, were both interested in the cultural scene. Sadhana remembers the dresses and material that were donated by her parents to the Annapurna B Group for costumes and stage props. Her father had noticed the way she would start dancing whenever music was played on the radio. And when an excited Babulal Doshi, a man from Gujarat, living just across the road in the same Oriya Bazaar, requested that Raj Gobinda admit his daughter to the newly opened dance school, he did not think twice. It was on 10 August 1952 that a new school, Kala Vikash Kendra, was inaugurated in a rented shop in Oriya Bazaar, owned by one Goura Ghose. Sadhana along with her cousin Basanti Bose and Goura Ghose's own sister, were the first three students of the Kendra. The first dance teacher of the Kendra, Mayadhar Rout, a 'hero' from the Annapurna B Group, and trained in the *gotipua* tradition, was appointed on a salary of Rs.15 per month; the monthly fee collected from the students was a rupee. The dance taught during the first ten years was a mixed fare of different styles; besides the few Odissi items, one could learn Bharatanatyam, Manipuri, Kathak and folk dances (snake and mayur dances).[2]

In the meanwhile the couple, Kelucharan and Laxmipriya, having left the Annapurna A Group, was trying to set up their home in Cuttack. Laxmipriya was quite in demand, both as a dancer as well as an actress, and for another ten years or so continued to be actively involved with the semi-professional theatre groups, which came into being in the early fifties, as well as with quite a few Oriya films. However, she had to give up dance in the end because of ill health most probably due to the fact that she had started dancing too soon after her daughter' s birth.

The Rupashree and Janata theatres, were branches funded by splinter groups of the two Annapurna Theatre groups along with individuals from other professions such as engineers and advocates who were interested in the theatre. The Rupashree Theatre Group initially operated from Khurda, about 30 km from Puri, and later shifted its activities to Cuttack. Here rehearsals were conducted in a godown at the College square. The Janata Theatre was set up about a year later and had its centre of activities in Banka

[2]According to a report in the *Ananda Bazar Patrika* dated 17 June 1954 during a special programme of dance and music organized by the Kala Vikash Kendra for the purpose of raising funds, 'there were a series of dance performances which included Kumari Sadhana Bose in *Dashavatara*, Prativa and Surama in Kathak, Minakshi Nanda in *Nataraja*, Prathiba Saho in Bharatanatyam, Jayanti in Odissi, Amala in Mayur and the girls of the Ranihat branch in a Santal dance. . . .'

Bazaar, in the erstwhile premises of the Orissa Theatres of Kalicharan Pattanayak.

Kelucharan involved himself with both these theatre groups more because it was useful for Laxmipriya; by now his interest had shifted increasingly towards dance. Through the private tuitions which were coming his way in increasing numbers, he started evolving a more systematic approach to what had emerged up until now under the still vague appellative of Oriya dance.

The cultural scene in Cuttack and Puri was lively and vibrant. Since the late forties state level dance competitions were being promoted in both the cities under the auspices of the Utkala Samaja. In addition, in 1943 a second institution—the National Music Association—devoted to the teaching of classical music had been set up in Cuttack. Although during the first few years only classes in vocal Hindustani music were held under Guru Kundara Adinarayan, by the early fifties the curriculum was expanded to include a drama and dance section, the dance teachers being Deva Prasad Das for Odissi and Chinmoy Lahiri for Kathak.

The Cuttack centre of All India Radio set up in 1948 was now headed by P.V. Krishnamurty, a dynamic man from the south, who acted as a promoter and catalyst to musicians, writers and dancers from all over Orissa. He was responsible for bringing together the three leading lights in the field of music, who, with their different backgrounds, enormous talent and scholarship, generated a revolution in the dance-music scene: Balakrishna Das from Puri district trained in the traditional Odissi music by Shyam Sundar Kar and Nrusinga Nath Kuntia as well as in Hindustani music by Bade Gulam Ali Khan of Calcutta; Bhubaneswar Mishra from Ganjam district, trained both in Karnatic as well as Hindustani classical music, and Hariprasad Chaurasia from Uttar Pradesh. With the support of the versatile Surendra Mohanty, the talented scriptwriter and dance teacher attached to the All India Radio as producer, Krishnamurty promoted both drama and dance-drama productions with the aim of improving the level of performing arts in general and to stimulate creativity among the artists.

Strangely enough it fell on a man from Gujarat to come under the spell of the charged cultural atmosphere of those years. In the mid forties, the political leader Jayaprakash

Babulal Doshi (sitting: centre), Kelucharan (sitting: second from left) and staff and students of Kala Vikash Kendra in the early 1970s.

Narayan sent his protégé Babulal Doshi to the newly constituted state of Orissa to spread the socialist message. On arrival, however, Babulal became so fascinated with the traditional forms of art he came across, that in the course of a few years not only did he forget all about his political mission, but also abandoned the lucrative jewellery business which he was managing along with his relatives and dedicated himself whole-heartedly to his newly discovered passion: the promotion and spreading of Odissi dance. Gifted with an extraordinarily strong will power and an open mind, it did not require much effort on the part of Babulal to involve in his crusade the most talented artists, scholars as well as politicians to achieve his objective. During the first few years his main preoccupation was to get enough money so as to house the Kala Vikash Kendra in its own building and for this he used all his resources. He even undertook a vow to go on a fast and subjected himself to austerities until the fund required could be collected. He succeeded in getting a piece of land on lease from the then Chief Minister Dr Harekrushna Mahatab in 1957, and along with Kalicharan Pattanayak set about collecting donations. He laid the foundation stone in August 1958 and completed the first floor of the building by December 1959. Earlier the classes were held in rented houses, first in Oriya Bazaar then in the Ganga Mandir, and from 1955 onwards in a two-storeyed building in Banka Bazaar.

It was during the second phase of the establishment, while the classes were being held in four rented shops in the Ganga Mandir, that Babulal requested Kelucharan to join the Kendra. After he joined the Kendra, Babulal Doshi acknowledged that the standard of teaching had been raised.[3] Kelucharan taught there on a regular basis from 1953 to 1965 and during this period he dedicated himself totally to the task of making the institution a vibrant centre for the propagation of the Odissi dance.

Kelucharan, after changing a couple of houses had settled down with his family in Kuthkhi Galli, a small lane near Sut Hata Bazaar not far from where Babulal Doshi was staying in Oriya Bazaar. The two rooms of the house were hared by him, his wife, their daughter, and by Mayadhar Rout, the other dance teacher at the Kendra. It was through the latter that Babulal came in touch with Kelucharan. Along with Kelucharan, most of his private students joined the institution: Champoka, Jayanti, Abha, Krishnapriya, Bonopriya, Susama, Pratima, Mira, Kadambari, Pratibha, Minakshi, Sanjukta and others. The number of students increased day by day. Soon the rented space became too small to accommodate the increasing number of small girls who were eager to learn. Another centre of the Kendra at Ranihat had to close down as it too became small to accommodate all the students.

By 1954, another deserter from the Annapurna B Group, Raghunath Dutta, joined the Kendra as an assistant in teaching dance. In the same year, a four-year dance curriculum was framed as a result of the collective effort of the teachers along with Kalicharan Pattanayak, who by now was devoting all his energies to the cause of dance as well as Nilamadhava Bose and Dayanidhi Das, both scholars attached to the Kendra.

Kelucharan was now working round the clock. Bonomali, his cousin (brother) from Raghurajpur, who had learned to play the mardala during his stay at the Annapurna A Group in Puri, was a source of constant support. Together they travelled between Cuttack and Chowdwar from one house to another on a ramshackle cycle, covering several miles a day giving private tuitions. Once a month Kelucharan would go to Angul, about 120 km from Cuttack, by train and spend 7-8 days at a stretch giving tuitions at several houses. Thrice a week he went by bus to Bhubaneswar to conduct dance classes in the Bhubaneswar Kala Kendra,

[3] Babulal Doshi, *Mo katha: Kala Vikash Kendra katha*, 1977.

Kelucharan performing the folk dance Kela Keluni with Laxmipriya (right) and Jayanti Ghosh (left).

the first institution of its kind which was founded in this fast developing 'new capital' in August 1955 by Anada Charan Das.

Kelucharan earned up to Rs. 900 per month from tuitions; he hardly ate or slept, keeping himself busy and forever on the move. In the evening, after the last tuition was over, if there were no rehearsals, he would watch the last show at a cinema hall and would never be back home before midnight. He would keep awake until the small hours, and would get his head massaged before falling asleep. In the morning, he would be up at eight, have a glass of *sharbat* and clad in a mended dhoti and kurta begin another hectic day of tuitions and rehearsals.

Besides the private tuitions and classes at the Kala Vikash

Kelucharan with Laxmipriya (right) and Krishnapriya (left) in Kela Keluni.

Kendra and the fortuitous collaborations with the Annapurna B Group, Kelucharan had to cope with requests for dance performances. He had stopped dancing himself and was more interested in projecting his students. From the early fifties his stage appearances became infrequent; he would occasionally perform the folk dance Kela Keluni (the snake charmer and his wife) from the Danda Nacha repertoire along with Laxmipriya and Jayanti or Krishnapriya as his two wives, and at times the *Dashavatara* in tandem with one of his students. But generally all his energy was directed towards promoting his young students. Besides conducting their rehearsals, he designed their dresses for the show, accompanied them on mardala and often had to sing due to a lack of vocal accompanists. The girls extremely young, between nine and ten years old, were suddenly getting more opportunities to perform on stage, either in the numerous dance competitions which were held in Puri and Cuttack sponsored by different organizations or at the annual functions of colleges and other institutions. There were also the annual dance-dramas presented by the Kala Vikash Kendra during its anniversary celebration in the

[4]Organized for the first time in 1952 by a group of young people in Cuttack, the festival was meant to celebrate the Kumara Purnima night, which marks the beginning of the holy month of *Kartika* with dance and music programmes. One of its main animators, Surendra Mohanty was responsible for the production of the dance-drama presented during the first few years. Each dance-drama used to be broadcast live by the All India Radio due to the active participation of the Director, P.V. Krishnamurty.

month of August, and those composed for the Kumara Utsava,[4] a festival held since 1952 in the month of October-November in Cuttack.

Although very young, the girls always gave their best. Among a host of children from all over India participating in the third annual function of the Children's Little Theatre, Sanjukta excelled with her ten-minute presentation of the Odissi piece '*Nahi ki koridela*' at the Imperial Theatre in Calcutta in May 1953. At the second anniversary function of the Kala Vikash Kendra held at the Nari Seva Sangh venue in August 1954,[5] Minakshi got a special mention from Rukmini Devi for her excellent presentation of the *Shiva Nataraja* dance (reworked by Kelucharan on the basis of the one performed by him in the *Devi Bhasmasura*). In 1955 Jayanti won the first prize at a dance competition in Puri with the performance of *Dashavatara* (which Kelucharan and Laxmipriya used to perform at the Annapurna Theatre). At the dance and music competition organized by the Nikhil Utkal Music Conference in Cuttack in April 1954, Sadhana Bose secured top position in the Odissi, Manipuri and Bharatanatyam dances in the age group of below 12 years. And Minakshi won a prize at the All Orissa Music Conference held in Cuttack under the Utkal Sangeet Samaj in March 1954.[6] During the Vasanta Utsava held in Calcutta at the Indian Association Hall in February 1954, among the Kala Vikash Kendra students who participated, Sadhana won a gold medal for her performance of the *Dashavatara*; on this occasion a short dance-drama, *Pausa Utsava* was also presented.[7]

It was during one of these competitions that an occasional remark from one of the participating teachers, left an indelible mark on Kelucharan's sensitive mind. Bono Bihari Maity originally from Calcutta, had been in Cuttack for quite a few years and used to teach a dance form known as Bangala Nacha. He was a follower of the Uday Shankar style and had first met Kelucharan and Laxmipriya in the late forties at the Annapurna B Group where he had taught them a dance piece on Shiva. A few years later some of his students were participating in a dance competition held at the Binapani School in Cuttack, where Sanjukta won the first prize while Maity's students did not get any. Put off by this, he asked Kelucharan in a rather contemptuous manner: 'Odissi? what is this "Odissi"? Never heard of it!'.

That was enough for Kelucharan, who at that very

[5] *Amrita Bazar Patrika*, 26 August 1954.
[6] *Statesman*, 1 April 1954.
[7] *Prajatantra*, 18 February 1954.

moment made a promise to himself that 'from now onward I will make every effort to show these fellows what this "Odissi" is'. Since then Kelucharan has never looked back and has worked single-mindedly to keep his promise all through life.

His commitment to the Kala Vikash Kendra was equally uncompromising; after the success of Sanjukta's dance at the Children's Little Theatre in Calcutta, almost every year Kelucharan's students, who took part in the function, always distinguished themselves (young Minakshi presented her ever popular item *Shiva Tandava* for three consecutive years; while the difficult acrobatic poses or *bandha* were the main attraction of the first part of the item it was always the *tandava* part with the gunpowder and coloured light effects which stole the show). More than once the director of the theatre, Samar Chatterji, had offered Kelucharan the post of a dance teacher—which he always refused—on a salary much higher than that at the Kendra (which started at Rs. 20 per month, gradually increasing to Rs. 35-Rs. 70-Rs. 150, to a maximum of Rs. 250).

Kelucharan also refused to teach Indrani Rehman, by then already a famous Bharatanatyam dancer. She approached him in Puri in May 1957 while he was rehearsing the dance-drama *Pancha Puspa*, written by Kalicharan Pattanayak, to be presented during the All Orissa Music Seminar organized by the Utkal Nrutya Sangeet Natyakala Parishad.

Indrani had first heard about the *devadasi* dance form of Orissa from her mother, Ragini Devi, back in the forties but could not get much information about this dance at that time. It was only after the participation of two university students from Orissa, Priyambada Mohanty and Dhirendranath Pattanayak, at the Inter University Youth Festival in Delhi in November 1954 with two Odissi dance sequences, '*Gumana kahinki*' (Why are you offended?) an Oriya song interpreted by the former, and the *Dashavatara* by the latter, that the existence of this dance form came to be acknowledged in the Delhi dance circles.

Indrani's efforts at learning the Odissi style continued. It was only through the intervention of Mayadhar Mansingh, an eminent Oriya poet and educationist, whom she had approached, that Indrani got an official invitation from the Orissa government to visit Orissa as a state guest in May 1957. Dr Mansingh had suggested to her that she could approach Kelucharan for the practical training in Odissi dance and Kalicharan Pattanayak for the theoretical aspects of it. She found Kelucharan in Puri in the green-room of the theatre where the performance was to take place the next day, and asked him straightaway if she could learn a few Odissi dance pieces from him. She had only 8 to 10 days at her disposal and she wanted to learn as much as possible in that short span of time. Kelucharan was taken aback by the request: that somebody could think that it was possible to learn the Odissi dance in such a brief period. Moreover, the Kala Vikash Kendra examinations were to start within a few days and he would not have been in a position to devote time to her that week.

Eventually she was able to pursuade Deva Prasad Das to give her lessons in Odissi. Since the early fifties he had been with the National Music Association and had recently joined the Bhubaneswar Kala Kendra as a full time teacher when Kelucharan stopped taking classes due to lack of time. It was due to the intervention of Ananda Charan Das, the secretary of the institution, that Deva Prasad was allowed to go thrice a month to Delhi to teach Indrani. Later on he travelled with her as an accompanist for dance performances in which her repertoire included Odissi pieces.

On the occasion of the second anniversary of the Kala Vikash Kendra in August 1954, besides the *Dashavatara* by Sadhana, the programme included Kathak dance by Pratima, *bhajan* by Balakrishna Das and *Sakhi Gopala*, a page from Orissa legends from the pen of Pundit Godavari Mishra and composed by Sri Nayan Kishor Mohanty.[8] In this short 20-minute dance-drama Sadhana and Mayadhar performed the roles of Krishna and Srivatsa respectively. The story is about the betrayal by a Brahmin named Narasingha, who promises to marry his daughter to the poor Srivatsa but does not honour it once he becomes rich. The pious Srivatsa gets Krishna as witness but on the way towards Narasingha's house he could not resist looking back to see if Krishna was following him, and finds the Lord transformed into a statue.

A dance-drama with the same name, 'Sakhi Gopala' was composed jointly by the two gurus, Kelucharan and Pankaj, for the Industrial Fair in Delhi in the winter of 1955, and dealt with the second part of the story.

After a temple is constructed around the statue of

[8] *Eastern Times*, 21 August 1954.

Krishna, the Lord appears in a dream to the *pujari* (enacted by Pankaj Charan) and tells him that he feels lonely without a statue of Radha near him. The *pujari's* daughter (Sadhana) is very devoted to the Sakhi Gopala Krishna (interpreted by Anuradha Mohanty, a student of Pankaj Charan from Puri) and comes to worship him every day. One day she falls ill and hence stops visiting the temple. And while she is recuperating at home, the king orders a statue of Radha be erected in the temple. The work is completed and when the *pujari's* daughter visits the temple the next time she notices the statue of Radha in the sanctum. On seeing her rival she dies out of jealousy and desperation and on her death her soul enters into the statue.

This second part of 'Sakhi Gopala', written by Kalicharan Pattanayak and set to music by Balakrishna Das, includes an invocation to Lord Ganesha '*Pada bande Gana Natha*' (I worship the feet of Lord Ganesh), composed specially for this occasion by Kelucharan; the dance was rendered by Priyambada Mohanty as *nartaki*. This dance-drama was, perhaps the first one to be entirely composed in the Odissi style, while the previous compositions had spurious elements in them.

In May 1954 a week-long celebration to mark the occasion of the Upendra Bhanja Jayanty was organized in Cuttack during which almost every day a different dance-drama was presented.[9] Among them was *Rutuchitra*, based on a selection of songs by Upendra Bhanja on the six seasons, composed by Kelucharan with his wife Laxmipriya as Labanyavati and Sadhana as *rutuvalika*.

With the collaboration between writers such as Surendra Mohanty, Kalicharan Pattanayak, Nilamadhava Bose, Nayan Kishor Mohanty and music directors such as Balakrishna Das, Bhubaneswar Mishra and P.V. Krishnamurty a number of dance-dramas were composed during this period, and this trend has continued since then.

After the departure of Mayadhar for Madras in 1955 to study Bharatanatyam and Kathakali at Kalakshetra, Kelucharan shifted to Durga Gudiani, a house in Oriya Bazaar, right in front of Babulal Doshi's residence. He lived in this house for almost four years. In the months prior to the annual examinations, some of the students residing outside Cuttack, would stay at Babulal Doshi's house and Kelucharan would train them there. Among them were Sanjukta, who came in summer from Madras, where she

[9] *Prajatantra*, 21 May 1954.

was studying Bharatnatyam at Kalakshetra; Sadhana, whose father had been posted to Berhampur (1954 onwards); and Vijay Pànda from Berhampur. At the same house Kelucharan taught the *Dashavatara* to Dhirendranath Pattanayak, a young student of Ravenshaw College, who was selected to participate in the 1954 Inter University Youth Festival in Delhi along with Priyambada Mohanty, also from the same college, accompanied on this occasion by her guru, Deva Prasad Das. Although not exactly the first performance of Odissi dance outside the state, it was however the first time that this graceful style came to the notice of scholars and critics and made its presence felt on the all-India dance scene.

Meanwhile, back in Orissa, everybody in the field of dance was getting busy. In the summer of 1955 Kelucharan literally spent his entire days and nights between the rehearsal rooms of Kala Vikash Kendra in Banka Bazaar and Babulal Doshi's house. The first version of *Virohi Chandrabhanu* (Deserted Chandrabhanu') was composed, with Sadhana as Labanyavati and Sanjukta as Chandrabhanu; the rehearsals would continue late into the night after which he would accompany the two girls to Babulal's house where they were residing, and continue to discuss with Kalicharan Pattanayak the meaning and interpretation of the intricate poetry of Upendra Bhanja.

This became a regular feature whenever Kelucharan was working on a new composition; not having received a formal education, he always needed to double-check the significance of each word and of the contextual meaning of a song with a learned person before interpreting its poetry into dance. Nilamadhava Bose recalls how Kelucharan would often make him sit in the rehearsal room to decide which choreographed version was most effective or what was the exact meaning of a particular word in a given context. This humility characterized Kelucharan all through his career; in the process of growing he has always been eager to learn more and to accept new ideas from whatever source at his disposal. He acknowledges the fact that:

> What I know and represent is only a drop in the ocean. Since I have not studied, the only language at my disposal is my *anga bhasa* (body language). For me it is important to maintain the link with the root from where this art has been derived; if the root is cut then the tree dies. It is essential to learn continually from the external world; the experience broadens as one is exposed to a

larger world. When I used to come back from my trips, my mother used to ask me 'Where have you been? How far is this place? Does the world end there or does it exist beyond that point?' And I used to answer that the world does not end because it does not have any beginning; it is a circle, a continuous circle. It starts and ends with you.

The people that I met in the course of collecting material for this book, remember Kelucharan with fondness, describing him as:

> 'humble, amiable and incredibly creative person',[10]
>
> 'extremely accommodating and adjusting, soft like butter',[11]
>
> 'sober and polite',[12]
>
> 'affectionate and tender',[13]
>
> 'courteous, dignified and hard working',[14]
>
> 'always eager to learn more. He would ask us again and again about the meaning of the Sanskrit "sloka" in the course of the composition of a new dance drama, never satisfied and for ever in search of knowledge',[15]
>
> 'an attractive and vulnerable personality',[16]
>
> 'patient, loving, pampering the students. He is gifted with an amazing sense of observation and penchant for details.'[17]

Govind Tej, an engineer turned scriptwriter and dance-drama director, although attached to the National Music Association, always preferred to work on his dance-dramas with Kelucharan: 'for his exceptional sensitivity in grasping the concept and suggestion contained in the script, his responsive mind and outstanding aesthetic sense'.

Their intense collaboration which lasted for about ten years between 1954 and 1964, produced some of the most interesting dance-dramas of the decade, which were composed for the annual presentation at the Kumara Utsava celebrations (and often repeat performances were held on behalf of the Kala Vikash Kendra). These included: *Urvashi* (1954), *Anadi Sangeeta* (Unending song) (1955), *Jibanara Chhanda* (Rhythms of life) (1957), *Krishna Gatha* (The story of Krishna) (1958), *Pancha Purnami* (Five full moon)

[10] Nilamadhava Bose.
[11] Ananda Charan Das.
[12] Samuel Sahu (Babi).
[13] Sadhana Bose.
[14] Priyambada Mohanty.
[15] Shanti Devi, who collaborated with Kelucharan in writing the scripts of several dance-dramas composed by him for the Shilabala Women's College at Cuttack.
[16] Sutapa Duttagupta.
[17] Rani Karnaa.

(1960), *Sri Jagannatha* (1961), *Amara Bharati* (Mother India) (1962), *Ambrapalli* (1964), and *Bharata Juddha* (Indian war) based on the *Mahabharata* (1965).

Some of the innovative elements in stage presentation, such as the cyclorama and the two-tier stage, were introduced in these dance-dramas, establishing a pattern which was followed more or less in all future presentations. The three stalwarts, Bhubaneswar Mishra who was in-charge of music, Govind Tej responsible for concept and script, and Kelucharan for dance would sit late into the nights working out in perfect unison the portions to be rehearsed the following day with the dancers. Often P.V. Krishnamurty would offer suggestions and insights, Chaurasia and Balakrishna Das would compose the music, dancers from different institutions would be recruited, and donations for the plays would generously pour in from different sources. The atmosphere was one of collaboration and goodwill among artists, conducive to the blossoming of creativity in each of the participants.

Among the dance-dramas composed by the Cuttack Kala Vikash Kendra's team in the mid-fifties were *Kishori Kanhu* (Radha Krishna) (1953), *Amrita Manthana* (Churning of the ocean) (1955), *Palli Gatha* (The ballad of countryside) and *Chitrangada* (1956), *Pancha Puspa* (Five flowers), *Nada Nupura* (The sound of ankle bells) and *Madana Bhasma* (The ashes of Madana) (1957), *Pujarini* (The lady who worships) (1958), *Meghadoot* (Cloud messenger) and *Kumara Sambava* (The birth of Kartika) (1959).

During the two years Kelucharan collaborated with the Bhubaneswar Kala Kendra, between 1955 and 1957, six dance-dramas were composed by him. All of them were written by Anada Charan Das and set to music by Balakrishna Das, also a music teacher at the Kendra. Among them, while the first dance-drama, *Ras Leela*, composed purely in the Odissi style, had the maximum number of performances the last one, *Jeevana Darshana*, an analogical deduction from the Buddhist philosophy of life, was perhaps the most ambitious as far as metaphorical expression was concerned.[18]

It was not possible for the young dancers to fully understand what they were trying portray while dancing; the subtle erotic meanings of the lyrics dealing with the Radha-Krishna theme were explained by Kelucharan in terms of childhood games among friends. Quite often he

[18] The other dance-dramas in order of composition are: *Jamuna puline* (On the bank of the Jamuna), *Bhasmasura badha* (The killing of demon Bhasma), *Shilpire swapna* (The artist's dream) and *Dhibara o nagakanya* (The boatman and serpent woman).

would have to wake them up, because oblivious of everything, between one scene and another during the show, some of the girls would fall asleep. For them it was more an excuse for missing school and having fun than any serious attempts at charting a career. Kelucharan looked after all of them like a father, dressing them for the show, doing their make-up and costume, and accompanying them back home.

Occasionally there were jibes and criticisms of the teaching of songs from the *Gita Govinda* or the *Kishora Chandrananda Champu*[19] to these young impressionable girls in view of their erotic content; but Kelucharan would most passionately argue that for him the *bhakti* element underlying each poem was so strong that there was no scope for any vulgarity or innuendoes.

For the *Krishna Gatha* dance-drama which was composed in 1958, an audition was held to select a dancer for the role of Krishna (Sadhana had been selected as Radha). The one who was chosen was Kumkum Das, a very naughty little girl who had joined the Ranihat branch of the Kala Vikash Kendra in 1954 at the age of eight. Her elder sister Mira had already received two years of training from Kelucharan in their house. Her classes in the beginning had been a disaster; she was just not bothered about dance. Kelucharan had to cajole her either by giving jasmine flowers for her hair or asking her to march like a little soldier. Within a couple of years the Ranihat branch had to be closed down because it was too small to accommodate all the students, and Kumkum joined other pupils at Banka Bazaar. The students attending the Odissi classes at this branch had the advantage of learning Kathak from Ram Gopal Krishna, a master from Calcutta who visited the Kendra twice a week.

In response to an advertisement in the Oriya newspaper, the *Prajatantra* of 22 June 1954 announcing the 'award of six stipends of Rs. 75 each per month for a period of four years with effect from July 1954 for higher training in music and dance in colleges for music and dance outside Orissa', both Sanjukta Mishra and Mayadhar Rout applied and were selected for the classes in Bharatanatyam and Kathakali at Rukmini Devi's Kalakshetra in Madras. Both of them would come back to Orissa during the summer vacations, Sanjukta to appear for her Odissi exams at the Kala Vikash Kendra and Mayadhar to resume his teaching. It was during their summer visits that the concept of *mudra* and *vinyoga* (hand

[19] A literary work written in the nineteenth century by Kavisurya Baladeva Ratha on the Radha-Krishna theme. The peculiarity of the poem lies in the fact that the first word would give you the letters of the Sanskrit language in an alphabetical order.

gestures and their applications) came to be discussed in a systematic way.

There is no doubt that their experience at Kalakshetra served as a sort of a blue print for Odissi in general and the Kala Vikash Kendra team in particular, which had been struggling for quite sometime to attain more methodical approach in the art of teaching and composing. The theoretical aspect of the Odissi style was far from codified and in this preliminary phase it was tempting to look around and draw inspiration from other dance forms in order to make it more systematic. The absence of common guidelines had already resulted in gurus training their students for dance competitions in fashions and styles based on their own understanding; there was no uniformity in terms of costume, repertoire, technique or interpretations. Each guru was acting on his own.

Scholars like Kalicharan Pattanayak, conducting research in the theoretical aspect with the aim of establishing clear-cut parameters for the Odissi style according to the dictates of the *Natya Shastra*, did not approve of the idea of having to borrow elements from the south, neglecting the guidelines contained in the indigenous manuscripts. But it is also a fact that till then none of the practitioners had ever seen any of these manuscripts; neither had any of them been published (the first Oriya translation of Nandikeswara's *Abhinaya Darpana*, compiled by Dhirendranath Pattanayak, was published in 1960).

It was clear that it had to be a collaborative effort, theoreticians on one side and practitioners on the other, to reach a certain degree of clarity and authenticity. The meetings among the gurus which started around 1957 in the open space at the Raghunath Mandir, in Telenga Bazaar, were urged by the need to share and pool in their accumulated knowledge and experiences with the aim of arriving at a mutual enrichment and a better understanding of the dance form.

During the first phase all the dance gurus were present: Deva Prasad, Pankaj Charan, Mayadhar, Kelucharan, Buda Chowdhury, Raghunath Dutta and Dayanidhi. Officially there was no connection between the Kala Vikash Kendra and Jayantika (the name by which this congregation came to be known).

The discussions began as an informal private affair. Slowly, however, they gained momentum and became known. When Dhirendranath Pattanayak, who had been awarded a scholarship by the Sangeet Natak Akademi for conducting research on Odissi dance after his dance debut in Delhi in 1954, also joined the group the discussions and demonstrations took on a new urgency. By the time they shifted to the drawing room of Lokanath Mishra, the *mangala charan* in honour of Lord Ganesha had already been composed with the approval of all the gurus. The initial *ukuta* or syllables recited by the mardala player were the ones Kelucharan had collected from Balabhadra Sahu and Agadu Maharana during his days at Raghurajpur. Other *bols* were composed on the spot.

While *mangala charan* was suggested by Dayanidhi Das, the very first stance of the dance, with the dancer opening up the hands in *pataka* and assuming a *chawka* position, was suggested by Dhirendranath Pattanayak. Pattanayak explains how he arrived at this decision:

> I was residing in Dimidesena village in Puri district for six months in 1959, to conduct research on the *gotipua* style of dance. During this period I came to know that a boy called Mulia belonging to a nearby village had earned the reputation of being a very good dancer. I immediately went and brought him to the house of the zamindar where I was residing. While watching his demonstration I noticed that he began the dance with the *ukuta* '*kadataka dhi dalla anga ta ta*', and by opening his two hands in 'ardhapataka' in a diagonal way. When we discussed all this during Jayantika I suggested that instead of *ardhapataka* we use the *pataka* hands opening them up in a horizontal way. This would not only have been in conformity with the definition of *natyarambhe* (starting of the dance) given in the *Abhinaya Darpana* but would also have suggested the standing pose of Lord Jagannath. At this point Kelucharan observed that '*kadataka dhi*' would have been too abrupt for a beginning and suggested instead '*tari kita dhi*' which were the *bols* collected by him from Raghurajpur.

The repertoire of the Odissi dance started to take shape in the image of a tree, beginning with the seed or *mangala charan*, to the trunk or *batu nrutya*, the efflorescence of the *pallavi*, the fruitfulness of the *abhinaya* and the falling of the leaves or *mokshia* at the end.

Rules and regulations were formulated regarding costumes, jewellery and hair styles based on texts like the *Abhinaya Chandrika* (written by Maheswara Mohapatra in the fifteenth century).[20] Notes were taken at every session by Dayanidhi and hung on a nail in Lokanath Mishra's

[20]It was during this time that, following the indications of the *Abhinaya Chandrika*, all the participants decided to adopt the *puspa chuda* style for the hair (hair arranged in a knot behind the head, surrounded by one or more strings of flowers and surmounted by a *tahia* or vertical crown). It so happened that for the staging of the dance drama *Meghadut*, produced in 1959 by the Kala Vikash Kendra, a costume designer from Puri came along to assist with the make-up and costume. At this point Dhirendranath Pattanayak, who was involved in the production, suggested that one could perhaps try to substitute the fresh flowers for the hair with a similar pattern made out of 'solo' pith (porous stem of a water creeper), the way they used to decorate the idols in Puri. Kelucharan sat with the artisan from Puri and designed for him the flower *bedha* (circle) and *tahia* which from then onward came to be used by the Odissi dancers.

drawing room wall and participants pledged to follow these rules by touching the earth as a solemn promise.

But divergences had already started to emerge with reference to the composition of the *batu nrutya*, a redefined version of the *thei ghara nata* of the *gotipua* (named as such because of the predominant '*thei*' *ukuta* in the rhythmic syllables of the *tala*). Deriving its name from *Batuk-bhairava*, the bachelor Shiva who is an adolescent and from the word *batuka* which refers to the neophyte at the time of his initiation, it incorporates all the main *bhangi* or basic postures of the style interlined with a variety of rhythmic combinations and is meant to illustrate the structural quality of the dance devoid of embellishments or elaborations. Keeping this basic quality in mind, it has been provided with a preliminary sequence which first introduces the musical instruments which accompany the dance, then the make-up and preparation of the dancer and finally the dance itself. Dhirendranath Pattanayak describes the reconstruction of the *batu* dance in the following passage:

> When I joined Jayantika the gurus mentioned about a *sola khanda vadya* (sixteen types of rhythmic variations) which were known as *batu*, but nobody was able to show it to me. So we reconstructed the present form on whatever scattered *bols* were availaible. The suggestion of starting with the basic poses depicting the dancer while playing the four musical instruments (veena, mardala, flute and manjira) was given by me.

Both Pankaj and Deva Prasad refused to follow this version, labelling it as Kelu's *gharana* and gradually stopped attending the meetings. Later on Deva Prasad composed a similar version calling it *sthai nata*.

Nevertheless the process continued; the dance in which equal importance was given to the elaboration of *swara* (melody) and *vadya* (rhythm) along with different combinations of dancing patterns was called *pallavi*, following the definition given in the *Abhinaya Chandrika*. The concluding piece in a dance recital which is based on intricate rhythmic combinations derived from the *gotipua vadya* tradition was named *mokshia*. Discussions on hand gestures and their uses were based on the indications contained in the *Abhinaya Darpana Prakasha*, an indigenous manuscript written by Jadunatha Singh in the seventeenth century, which was in the possession of Kalicharan Pattanayak. Dance demonstrations by students were arranged as part of the meetings and also for the general

At the All-India Dance Seminar in Madras, 1958, from right (sitting): Kelucharan, Balakrishna Das; and (standing) Sanjukta Mishra and Kalicharan Pattanayak.

public at the Nari Seva Sangh in Cuttack, in September 1959 and again in June 1960. Kelucharan by then had already composed three *pallavis*: the first in the Raga Basanta, set to music by Balakrishna Das based on the tune of the traditional Odissi song '*Shyamo ja ja juhara to pirati ki*' (Go away, oh unfaithful Shyamo), the second in the raga Kalyani based on the tune of the Oriya song '*Dekhiba para asare prana sangini*' (Oh friend, come and watch), and the third in the Raga Mohana set to music by Bhubaneswar Mishra.

During this period he also composed *abhinaya* for Oriya songs like '*Bhangi chanha*' (Look at his triple-bent pose) by Kavisurya Baladeva Ratha, '*Ki nadore prana sangini*' (What a beautiful sound, oh friend) by poet Gopala Krishna and '*Bibhusana puspe ja kanti jana*' (The lady whose complexion is resplendent like a flower) by Upendra Bhanja, and the Sanskrit song from the *Gita Govinda* '*lalita labanga lata*' (Soft clove creepers). Some of these pieces were demonstrated by his students on behalf of Jayantika.

In January 1958 Kelucharan accompanied Kalicharan Pattanayak to Madras on the occasion of the All-India Dance Seminar held during the 31st Conference of the Music Academy.[21] On behalf of the Kala Vikash Kendra Sanjukta danced to the song '*lalita labanga lata*' accompanied by Kelucharan on the mardala and Balakrishna Das

[21] *The Hindu*, 3 January 1958.

The Odissi troupe that gave a performance in the Dance Seminar of the Sangeet Natak Akadami in New Delhi.

Participants to Sakhi Gopal dance-drama in Delhi in 1955 (see p. 92).

as vocalist while Kalicharan read a paper on the historical and practical aspects of the Odissi.

Again on 5 April 1958, the same team, with Jayanti Ghosh instead of Sanjukta (she was not availaible at the time), gave a demonstration of Odissi dance in New Delhi during the All-India Dance Seminar organized by the Sangeet Natak Akademi at the Vigyan Bhawan.[22] On this occasion Kalicharan read a paper on the classical aspects of the Odissi dance and Jayanti presented a single dance sequence including *mangala charan*, *batu*, *dekhiba para asare* and *mokshia*, accompanied by Kelucharan on the mardala. She wore the sari in Chandana Jatra style (similar to the one worn by the *gotipuas* while dancing on a red boat on the occasion of the Chandana Jatra) with the *pallu* of the sari made to hang in front between the thighs. The dancer wore silver ornaments on her head, neck, arms and the waist. A day earlier Nandita Mohanty accompanied on the mardala by guru Mahadev Rout gave a demonstration of Odissi on behalf of the National Music Association. The occasion

[22] *Samaja*, 29 April 1958.

was considered to be a historic one for the Odissi dance. According to Kalicharan Pattanayak: 'From what the chairperson of that meeting announced that day, everybody came to know about "Odissi" receiving the fifth position among the classical dance styles of India.'[23]

A step towards recognition of Odissi as a classical dance style had already been taken at the time of the 3rd Inter University Youth Festival held in Delhi in 1956. During the 1st Youth Festival in 1954 a young and nervous Priyambada, in spite of the success of her 8-minute performance, had to content herself with a third prize because of the unknown dance form she was presenting.

However, during the 3rd Inter University Festival not only did she get the first prize (and Susuma Tej, another Odissi dancer from Orissa the second prize) but at the end of the performance (which was allowed to last for full 15 minutes although the allotted time for each participant was only 8 minutes) an enthusiastic group of young participants literally lifted Kelucharan on their shoulders and carried him all around the camp in a triumphant procession. These were the same boys (all participants from the Lucknow University in the Kathak style) who were so captivated by the dance during the rehearsals that they did not allow the time keeper to press the bell at the end of the 8 minutes so that Priyambada could complete the *Kalyani pallavi* followed by '*Dekhiba para asare*'.

In March 1959 Odissi on behalf of the Kala Vikash Kendra was presented among the five classical dance styles (Kathak, Manipuri, Bharatanatyam and Kathakali) at the All India Dance Festival in Calcutta organized by Nritya Bharati. Kumkum Das and Krishnapriya Nanda danced a Radha-Krishna duet accompanied by Kelucharan on the mardala.[24]

In the middle of all this activity, the meetings of Jayantika continued. In one of these meetings, held in the new building of the Kala Vikash Kendra in July 1959, the following resolutions were passed: to establish a research wing under the banner of Jayantika, for conducting research on Odissi and folk dances; to ask the Orissa Sangeet Natak Akademi to provide assistance for this project; and a fortnightly report from research scholars to be submitted to Jayantika.[25]

It was some time during this period that Kelucharan suffered an attack of tuberculosis; he had just started

[23] *Samaja*, 24 April 1958.
[24] *Samaja*, 27 March 1959.
[25] *Prajatantra*, 21 July 1959.

composing the first stanza of an *ashtapadi* from Jayadeva's *Gita Govinda*, '*nindati chadanam*' (She slanders sandal-balm), when streaks of blood appeared in the sputum. Strangely enough whenever he attempted to compose this particular *ashtapadi* some misfortune or the other would befall him, the latest being the bypass surgery he had to undergo in April 1990, just after having composed part of it for some senior students. 'I think Lord Jagannath does not want me to compose this song for him!' says Kelucharan.

The news of Kelucharan's illness spread faster than the diagnosis itself; the doctor who visited him had not yet given his final verdict, but already there were letters from students requesting the doctor to cure their guru quickly. Voluntary donations started to pour in; Rs. 5,000 donated by the students of the Girls High School where he used to teach, one month's salary of Rs. 250 was advanced to him by the Kala Vikash Kendra, the central Sangeet Natak Akademi sanctioned Rs. 1,000 (of which only half was paid because by the time the first instalment reached him, he was already cured) and Laxmipriya, his wife, sold her gold ornaments for Rs. 2,000.

For about three to four months he had to take complete rest; all his activities, classes, tuitions, rehearsals, performances were totally stopped. Above all he had to give up the habit of smoking bidis, a habit which he had picked up while working at the betel leaf plantation; he had become a chain-smoker. The doctor had been so strict in this regard that Kelucharan would wake up suddenly at night with the fear of having started smoking again.

By this time Kelucharan and his family had moved to a house in Peyton Sahi, not far from where the other Odissi guru, Deva Prasad Das, lived. Famous for his comic roles during the years he was with the Orissa Theatres and the Annapurna A Group he now considered his duty to visit Kelucharan every afternoon and keep him in good spirits with his jokes. His favourite one was of the squint-eyed person; he would start by telling Kelucharan:

How lucky you are! Sitting here the whole day long and getting fat by eating all this good food, while everything goes wrong with me. I have a wife who squints, my dog has become cross-eyed too; the hen has lost one eye and the bed where I sleep has a leg shorter than the others. The plate from which I eat is crooked and my students paid me only three tuition fees instead of eight; and on top of all this when I lie down at night and look at the moon I see that she is crooked too.

This comic narrative would be accompanied by exquisite acting and hilarious facial expressions!

Kelucharan was on a very rich diet, consisting of ghee, milk and fruit juice and had managed to gain 20 kg during the first phase of his recuperation; when his weight increased to 65 kg the diet had to be revised. He had become so fat that Ramani, who had come all the way from Bhadrak to learn Odissi from him, was hardly able to recognize him. Ramani had been introduced to him recently at All India Seminar at Bhadrak which Kelucharan had attended along with the Kala Vikash Kendra team. The young boy, who had learnt a variety of dance styles and was teaching at a local institution in Bhadrak, was fascinated by the demonstration of Odissi at the seminar and had made up his mind to go to Cuttack and learn from Kelucharan.

When finally Ramani was able to shift he found that Kelucharan had discontinued his classes due to his illness and had no clue where to find him. He met his prospective teacher quite by chance. While walking in Peyton Sahi one day, he saw somebody, vaguely resembling the person whom he had met in Bhadrak, sitting in a chair outside a house, but the thin moustaches and the fat figure were deceptive. It was Kelucharan who recognized him and called him over. The training started almost that same day, although not immediately as far as dance was concerned, because Kelucharan was not supposed to tire himself, but in tabla. Ramani remained from that day onward one of the most faithful among his male students. During the entire period of his training at the Kala Vikash Kendra he was like a son to Kelucharan, helping him and his family almost daily and receiving from his guru not only lessons in dance but also in all aspects of life.

Kelucharan resumed work after about six months, in full form and totally reinvigorated, surrounded more than ever by the affection and support of his numerous students. He found a substitute to the forbidden bidis in betel leaves and from now on a *kada pan* (betel leaf stuffed with tobacco and other aromatic ingredients) box would always be by his side, dutifully filled by his wife. For some years, in the early sixties, he found inspiration for his compositions in the smoking of *ganja* (dry leaves of the cannabis plant); its intoxicating effect further stimulated his already fertile imagination. However, this habit did not last long ; he soon realized that there was no need to take any stimulant to be creative in dance.

During Kelucharan's absence because of illness there was hardly any progress on the Jayantika front; slowly each of the participants started to get assignments in and outside Orissa, which kept them busy and the meetings of the group became less frequent. The resolution to convert the association into a permanent academy, where students could learn from different gurus all assembled under one roof, never materialized, and the work undertaken remained unfinished, never again to be resumed with the same openness of mind and spirit of cooperation from its participants.

Meanwhile the work with the Kala Vikash Kendra plus the private programmes with his students kept Kelucharan extremely busy. New solo compositions as well as new dance-dramas were composed by him in the early sixties. For Priyambada's performance in Delhi in 1961 (organized by the Little Theatre Group at Sapru House) a total of eleven dance peices were rehearsed, all presented by her in separate sequences. Among the new items that were composed by Kelucharan for this occasion were two *ashtapadis 'yami he kamiha saranam'* (Whom can I seek for refuge) and *'pashyati dishi dishi rahasi bhabantam'* (In her loneliness she sees you everywhere) and two Oriya songs, *'Shyamaku juhara tara premaru juhara'* (I salute Krishna and his love) by Gopala Krishna and *'Tora sharana gallire Murali'* (I come to you for protection, oh Krishna) by Bonomali. Another *ashtapadi, 'yahi Madhava yahi Keshava ma bada kaitaba badam'* (Go away Madhava, go away Keshava, don't tell your lies to me), was composed in the same year for Sanjukta.

All these compositions, especially the *ashtapadi* from the *Gita Govinda*, were continuously elaborated upon by Kelucharan; they grew along with him and became richly chiselled masterpieces imparted to hundreds of students through the years and finally attained their full beauty by his own stage interpretations in the late eighties.

For the time being the first versions of these compositions were just linear interpretations of the poetry, interspersed here and there with repetitions of the same line rendered by different *mudras* but not yet amplified by the inclusion of *sanchari* or enlarged interpolations. For example, in the *ashtapadi 'pashyati dishi dishi'* (She sees you everywhere), whose meaning was explained to Kelucharan by Pundit Banambara Acharya while the composition was in progress in Priyambada's house with the music set to raga Bhairavi by Balakrishna Das, it was only in the second stanza, where Radha is described stumbling every few steps in her haste to meet Krishna, that while the line *'patati padani kiyanti chalanti'* (she stumbles after a few steps) was repeated, different ways of falling were shown.

A far cry from the version that Kelucharan himself presented in Delhi in 1996 during a private function organized by the art collector O.P. Jain; here he dwelt on the first line *'pashyati dishi dishi'* for more than 10 minutes, literally searching for Krishna everywhere, coming down from the stage—which had gone totally dark due to a sudden load-shedding—and mixing among the public, asking them if they had seen him, mistaking him for the dark shadows created by the moonlight, embracing the trees, addressing the clouds in his passionate search for the beloved, and then returning to the stage with the coming back of the light and continuing with the rest of the song.

The *ashtapadi 'yahi Madhava, yahi Keshava'* did not include at this stage the mischievous responses of Krishna to the string of accusations of infidelity hurled by Radha on seeing the marks left by the other woman on his body. His lies about having gone in search of flowers in the forest and having been scratched by thorns (no, these are not nail marks from another woman!) and having had his lips smeared by the black juice of berries and not by kissing the rival's kohl filled eyes were all missing in the version composed for young Sanjukta in 1961.

It took some more years before the 'solo' compositions were extended to enable a more dramatized interpretation; this happened gradually along with the maturity of the dancers and the development of Kelucharan as a composer. A step in this direction was the first staging of the *Gita Govinda* as a dance-drama composed by Kelucharan in 1961 for the Kala Vikash Kendra. This first version had Sanjukta as Radha and Mayadhar as Krishna. It is possible that the larger scope for characterization of the dance-drama form may have influenced the extended versions of the subsequent solo *abhinaya* pieces. It is equally possible that

Mayadhar's exposure to the Bharatanatyam and Kathakali dance styles, with elaborated *abhinaya* compositions, may have inspired the Odissi gurus to enlarge the scope of their own versions. However, one should not underestimate the experience that Kelucharan had gained in the rich milieu of the Ras Leela theatre, with its vast reservoir of dramatized songs replete with colourful facts and anecdotes from Krishna's epic, and which must have been an unending source of inspiration for all his future compositions.

Among the other dance-dramas composed by Kelucharan for the Kala Vikash Kendra in the early sixties were: *Braja Leela* (The sports at Braja) (1961), *Ramayana* (1961), *Tapaswini* (The lady who performs penance) (1962), *Chandrabhaga* (1962), *Vikrama Urvashi* (1963), *Shakuntala* (1963), *Bhanu Sinhara Padavali* (songs by Bhanu Sinhara) (1964) and *Krishna Leela* (1964). Some of these dance-dramas were presented with a large number of artists and elaborate stage settings. For the *Ramayana* ballet more than 70 artists were employed and for the first time a revolving stage was used. It was a three-day show and had Kumkum in the role of Sita and Mayadhar as Rama.

For the dance-drama *Tapaswini*, which was staged on the occasion of the centenary celebrations of the Oriya poet Gangadhar Meher, a gorgeous set consisting of four stages, two of them fixed and two rotating, was set up and more than a hundred artists were involved. The idea of the revolving stages had been suggested by Mayadhar, who had just returned from a ten-month course in stagecraft with the Natya Ballet Centre in Delhi. The stages were made to rest on two pairs of bullock-cart wheels, each being 12 ft in diameter, with small wheels under them and were supposed to be moved by a motor, but when finally the motor did not work, they had to be rotated manually (a similar device, in a very rudimentary form, was also used by some Jatra groups for revolving the idols during a show).

During the composition of this dance-drama, as in most of the others composed for the Kala Vikash Kendra, Kelucharan was assisted by Mayadhar, who besides interpreting some of the major male roles, was also responsible for stage setting, costumes and conducting rehearsals in Kelucharan's absence. Mayadhar had a lot of respect for Kelucharan who was senior to him in age, and would usually not interfere with his compositions; the two would conduct their own classes (Mayadhar taught both

Bharatanatyam and Odissi) and had their own students.

Since 1957 the Kala Vikash Kendra had been receiving financial help from the central Sangeet Natak Akademi for conducting research on the folk and tribal dances of Orissa and over years had organized more than one research trip to the tribal areas of Kalahandi, Koraput and Bolangir to study the dances of the local communities.

The Kala Vikash Kendra team, headed by Kelucharan, would spend a considerable period of time in each village armed with a tape recorder, a still camera and pen and paper to record and note down the rhythms, songs and steps of each dance. Kelucharan was often seen dancing with the tribal girls, playing changu with the tribal boys and sharing food with them. Following these research expeditions the first few monographs on tribal and folk dances of Orissa were published by the Kala Vikash Kendra in the early sixties and these dances were taught to the students of the institution.

Kelucharan was exposed to the martial Chhau dance of Mayurbhanj in the late forties when, during his brief return to the Annapurna A Group in Puri, he met the visiting

Kelucharan (playing changu*) with Adivasis of the Koraput area in south Orissa.*

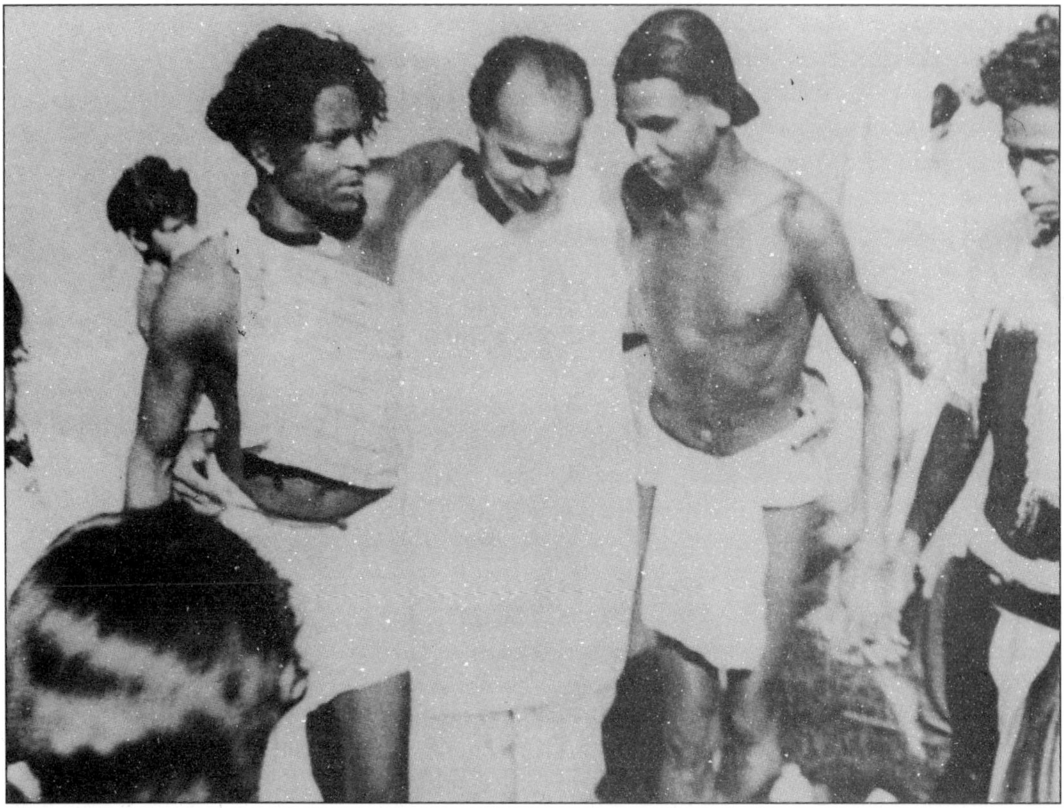

Dancing with Adivasis.

drama troupe from Baripada headed by Ram Chandra Das, an Inspector General of police cum drama director cum manager of the Uttar Sahi team of Chhau dancers (Kelucharan remembers how Ram Babu after having seen his rendering of the *Dashavatara*, pointed out two of his defects: an uncontrolled raising of the shoulders and an equally involuntary movement of the eyebrows). Kelucharan had been asked by Ram Babu to help set up the stage for a drama performance and on this occasion he had the opportunity to see the *Shiva Tandava* sequence in the Chhau style by Shri Hari Nayak, the star performer among the Baripada Chhau dancers. Keeping this piece in mind Kelucharan later reworked the original *Shiva Nataraja* dance on a similar pattern, maintaining the triple division of *srusti* (creation), *sthiti* (preservation), *pralaya* (destruction) and substituting the vigourous and masculine Chhau movements with steps more akin to the Odissi style.

Similarly, at the Annapurna A Theatre, when a drama on the life of Buxi Jagabandhu[26] was being staged and Kelucharan played the part of a *paika*,[27] he had an opportunity

[26] Leader of the revolt against British rulers, which started in the town of Khurda in 1817 and spread all over the central and coastal parts of Orissa by 1820.

[27] From the word *padatika* or 'infantry soldiers', they constituted more than 50 per cent of the population of Orissa; farmers by profession, they used to defend the boundaries of the kingdoms during wars maintaining themselves fit during peace by practicing acrobatics and several mock fights with different weapons.

to learn the martial art steps along with some of the fighting techniques of the style. This exposure to different body movements enriched his vocabulary and proved useful while composing dance-dramas in the later years.

In December 1964 the Kala Vikash Kendra organized a grand three-day show in Bombay at Biraja Matrushree Gruha, with more than a hundred artists from Orissa. The performances included folk dances by the Bhagawan Sahu troupe, Mayurbhanji Chhau by the Baripada artists, *gotipua* dance by artists from Puri and the dance-drama *Krishna Leela* by the Kala Vikash Kendra team. In order to stage this production Kelucharan had to work constantly for seven days and nights. After which he had to travel to Bombay, conduct stage rehearsals, get the girls ready and accompany them on the pakhawaj. Without any sleep or rest it was so tiring that at the end of it, Kelucharan collapsed and was down with high fever for several days.

This was, and remained all through his career, his way of working: oblivious of time, physical needs or hardships, feeding only on betel leaves and creative inspiration. He has a tremendous capacity to immerse himself totally, body and soul, into work—any type of work be it a dance composition, a repair work for the house, cleaning the gutter or teaching a newcomer. Kelucharan does his work with utmost care and penchant for details. Perhaps the most amazing thing is that in a group activity, he always succeeds in carrying along with him other people involved as if infecting everybody with his own energy and enthusiasm.

Already in those years Kelucharan devoted his time to different activities simultaneously; there were classes at the Kala Vikash Kendra, private tuitions, dance performances of students, composition of dance-dramas, new solo compositions, demonstrations at dance seminars to mention just a few, and everything was attended to with total commitment.

Among all these, the work for the Kala Vikash Kendra, although not adequately remunerative, was nevertheless the most engaging one; he had given up other offers only to be able to dedicate his time and energy to make this institution most effective. He shared with Babulal Doshi an unrestricted enthusiasm towards the same goal; both were driven by an identical obsession which till that point of time had been able to absorb all misunderstandings. With the increasing popularity of Kelucharan as a dance guru, through the frequent stage appearances of some of his students, the Kendra too was gaining fame and recognition.

Till the early sixties the Kendra functioned as the most vibrant venue for the congregation of gurus, musicians and artists involved in revival of Odissi; but by the mid sixties other institutions emerged and many of the artistes moved to new locations. Musicians such as Balakrishna Das and Bikhari Bala joined the newly established Utkal Sangeet Mahavidyalay at Bhubaneswar; Rakhal Mohanty got a job at the All India Radio in Cuttack and Mayadhar Rout left Orissa for Delhi in 1967.

Kelucharan was getting restless and was feeling tied down by the encumbrances. He wanted more freedom to move around so that he could spread his knowledge of dance to as many students as possible all over India. Besides, he became the target of malicious accusations which he considered unjust and unwarranted. His success gave rise to jealousies. One day Babulal mentioned to him that he had overheard comments like 'we slog and he gets the money' hinting at his increasing engagements outside the Kendra. Kelucharan decided to quit, although he did not altogether sever his links with the Kendra. Within a couple of years, around 1967, he introduced condensed courses during summer months which allowed for intensive teaching thereby enabling the participants to practice full-time. It also gave him the freedom to be as mobile as possible.

DANCING THROUGH HIS DISCIPLES

THE FAMILY was residing in a small house in Peyton Sahi when Kelucharan fell ill. They had shifted here after a brief stay in a rented house in Meria Bazaar. By this time he had already started looking for a small plot, where he could one day build his own house. During his stay at Meria Bazaar one of his relatives showed him a marshy piece of land of about 60 X 50 ft on sale in Samanta Sahi, an area not far from the Cuttack bus stand. He had started saving earnestly so as to collect the necessary amount of Rs. 1,500 for purchasing the land. But it was only after recovering from his illness about a year later that, with the left over money and a loan from the Kala Vikash Kendra, he was finally able to buy the land.

Soon after 1961, he shifted to a room in the compound of Khuntia's house to be able to supervise the construction work. Khuntia was a milkman by caste, who lived on the other side of the small lane where the land was located; no other house had yet been built in that area. The room where Kelucharan and his family resided for about four years before shifting to their new house, had an asbestos roof and a huge coconut tree on its side. The land was in a very low-lying area and was virtually flooded throughout the year. Kelucharan remembers how he would often go over there for fishing and proudly bring back the catch for the entire family. One day an exceptionally big catch pulled very hard at the fishing line sending Kelucharan into the water. That brought his fishing career to an end.

Before building the house a considerable amount of sand filling was required in order to raise the level of the land; the work was not easy as the marshy ground made it difficult for the trucks to operate in that area. One day, after a particularly heavy rainfall, a heavily loaded truck sank deep into the mire and would not move. Kelucharan had to pay Rs. 1,000 to the driver to arrange for another truck to tow it out and as reimbursement for all the parts which broke in the process. At the end of it, he was left with only a hoe in his hands, given by the driver as a token of compensation. He was without a single penny and had to borrow again from the Kala Vikash Kendra to be able to proceed with the construction work.

Within two months the preliminary structure of bamboo and wooden planks was destroyed twice by two subsequent downpours. During the first cyclonic storm, the situation in the entire *sahi* was desperate. In the midst of flying roofs and debris, for two nights, Kelucharan and his family survived clutching the coconut tree in their compound. On the third day the entire family, carrying the belongings over their heads, had to shift to Sanjukta's house and stayed there for a week. In the process many documents, including Laxmipriya's prize certificates, got washed away. During the second cyclone, Kelucharan was on a tour of Rourkela in the western part of Orissa. On his return, he found that, of the entire structure, only a lonely post with a vulture perched on top of it was left standing. He started building all over again, this time with bricks and cement; he built the first two rooms of the house, the kitchen and Charu's room, with a thatched roof, and the two bedrooms with a concrete one.

Kelucharan's first handling of construction material (*chuna* or lime instead of cement since this was not in use then) goes back to the time when, for few months before starting work at the *panna baraja*, he helped his maternal uncle, Arthabanda Maharana, in the construction of a temple.

Since then the fascination remained and one could say that, all through Kelucharan's life, the passion for brick and cement 'compositions' runs as an undercurrent to his primary passion for dance. Similar concentration and research aptitude can be seen at work whether he is building an attic, raising a boundary wall, planning the extension of the building or counting the beats of a rhythmic

Kelucharan tries his hand at masonry.

composition. Each type of work is a new discovery and the solutions found each time, are directly derived from the practical study of each situation. Extremely observant and alert, the beam structure observed in a roof in Bombay would become the source of inspiration for the construction of the ceiling of his house, without having to consult any structural engineer!

His way of relating to the masons is interesting; he literally becomes one of them, sharing their work, mixing the cement, joining the bricks, casting the roof, plastering the walls and also keeping the work going on his own in their absence.

During the construction of the dance hall, which was undertaken years later in the early seventies, Kelucharan decided to build a false ceiling, which would be entirely made of bamboo; the task was not easy because the bamboo had to be tightly intertwined and the entire structure had to be self-supporting. The mason refused to do it, complaining that the bamboo provided for the job was of inferior quality. Kelucharan took up the challenge and vowed that he will be able to complete the entire ceiling

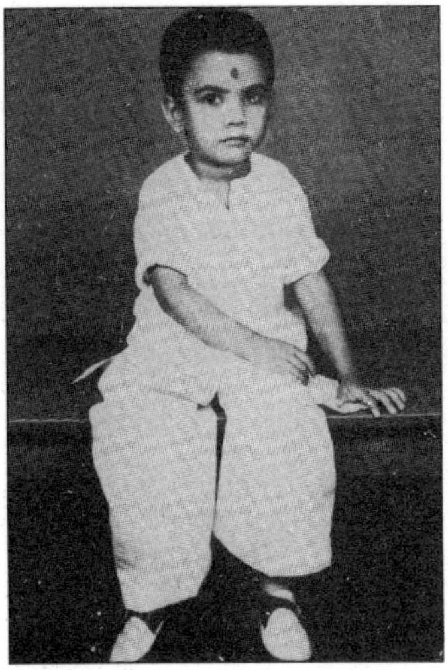

Three years old Ratikanta.

with the same bamboo in four days. The mason could not believe his eyes when he returned after four days and found the work neatly executed by Kelucharan!

While the floor was being laid, he taught the workers the technique of designing a white lotus at the centre of the cemented surface. He cut a piece of folded paper into the shape of a petal. He then unfolded it and placed it at the centre of the floor. After it had been traced on the wet cement, the inside of the petals were scooped out and filled with white cement. In this way he created the beautiful *bindu* in the middle of the dance floor which was a witness to the blossoming of so many dancers in the years to come.

The *ghara* (space for worship) was constructed soon after the family moved into the new house around 1965. Their son, Ratikanta, was born in the same year and it was for his first ceremony, twenty-one days after the birth, that the small temple in one corner of the inner courtyard was built. The place had been a natural choice, for soon after purchasing the field, Kelucharan had seen a snake at that very spot; months later, the snake reappeared, again at the same place, while the foundations were being laid. The wooden door posts and the door for the small temple-house

Kelucharan, Siri Nani and Laxmipriya at their Cuttack residence in the late 1970s.

were prepared by Kelucharan; he planed the wood, inlaid it and polished it before fixing it to the walls. From now on the puja to Lord Jagannath was performed regularly in the house; the idol of Lord Jagannath, along with that of His brother Balabhadra and sister Subhadra, were brought from the village by Kelucharan's mother when she came to stay with them in Cuttack.

One day towards the end of 1966, when Kelucharan was up on a scaffolding, in order to construct a shelf in Charu's room, he received a telegram from Delhi. Holding it in his hands still smeared with cement, he went to the neighbour to get it translated. He was dumbfounded finding that he had been chosen by the Sangeet Natak Akademi for the National Award in the dance category.

The function was to be held in Delhi towards the beginning of January 1967 and the award was to be presented by Prime Minister Indira Gandhi. It was for the first time that an artist of the Odissi dance form was being given the award. His father's words came back to him, and with tears in his eyes he went to prostrate himself in front of the image of Lord Shiva, offering a silent tribute to all his gurus, Balabhadra Sahu, Mohansundar Dev Goswami, Dayal Sharan and Pankaj Charan Das. He felt that the award should have been conferred on them first rather than on him; he accepted it for the sake of Odissi and considered himself just a humble *sevaka* at its altar.

'Kelucharan was overwhelmed with joy on hearing the news', observed Dhirendranath Pattanayak, who was at that time a member of the Sangeet Natak Akademi and one who had most strongly recommended Kelucharan's name for the award.

One day I had called him home asking him to give me his curriculum vitae. Since he did not have one ready, I wrote it down for him without telling him the purpose for which it was needed. So, to him, the award was totally unexpected. He ran to my house with the telegram in his hands and embraced me with tears in his eyes. That first award gave him a great deal of confidence.

At the award function in Delhi, Kelucharan did not dance but accompanied on the pakhawaj his most gifted student Sanjukta, whose performance included the *batu* and the *ashtapadi 'pashyati dishi dishi'*, with Balakrishna Das lending vocal support.

Another major event which was scheduled for March

of that year in Delhi was the seminar on poet Jayadeva's *Gita Govinda*, jointly organized by the Sangeet Natak Akademi and the Lalit Kala Akademi. The *Gita Govinda* celebration, aimed at presenting music, dance and paintings based on the exquisite poem. Scholars and dancers drawn from all classical styles were invited to participate with their versions of Jayadeva's *ashtapadi*.

Before the seminar, two new *ashtapadis* were composed in the Odissi dance form at Kumkum's parents house, located near the Chandi Mandir in Cuttack. Kelucharan would sit late into the night, discussing the meaning of the verses of the two lyrics, '*sakhi he Kesimathanamudaram*' (Oh sakhi, bring the killer of the demon Kesi) and '*dhira samire Yamuna tire*' (a soft breeze blows on the bank of the river Yamuna) with the Sanskrit pundit Panchanana Kar, who used to visit their house. Kumkum's mother would write down the meaning in Oriya for Kelucharan to read it at home.

It was always a problem finding a cycle rickshaw so late in the night and often Kelucharan would have to walk back all the way, reaching home almost at dawn; along the way the vision of Krishna in different poses—reclining on the bed of flowers, collecting the tender leaves for Radha, watching anxiously towards the path for her arrival, suggested by the whispering wind—would play on his mind. The next day many of these would be incorporated in the dance composition.

The whole family would be involved; Kumkum's mother would want to know the type of *pitha* (sweet pancake) she should prepare for the next day and the father would sit next to Kelucharan and offer his suggestions. But the one person who was totally unconcerned was Kumkum. She would faithfully copy whatever movements were shown by Kelucharan without participating in the discussions as if she were only going through the motions. (Once she did ask about the meaning of '*pinapayodhara mardanacancala-karayugasali*'[1] and finding no response from any quarter, she decided to keep quiet from that day onwards).

One day, while they were at work on the composition, Kalicharan Pattanayak dropped in to check if what was being composed would be in consonance with his speech at the seminar. After having seen the '*dhira samire*' piece, he asked Kelucharan about the sources from which he had taken the Krishna poses visualized in the dance. Kelucharan answered

[1] 'With restless hands that squeeze full breasts of cowherdesses' (from the eleventh verse of song '*dhira samire Yamuna tire*').

that being a *chitrakara pua* it was not difficult for him to relate to those poses. Kalicharan invited him to his house the next day and as soon as he entered, placed before him a voluminous *tala-patra* full of illustrations, and said to him: 'Now I will see if you are really a *chitrakara pua*; just tell me how old is this manuscript?'

The manuscript contained verses from the *Gita Govinda*; Kelucharan offered *pranam* to the *pothi* by bringing it repeatedly to his forehead and in front of his chest and started looking at the illustrations very closely; he found there the very poses that he had used in the dance composition. Then taking a drop of sweat from his forehead he rubbed it on one of the illustrations; observing the colour fade he replied, 'Not more than 2-3 years old.' Kalicharan gave him another manuscript for inspection and asked the same question; this time Kelucharan, after repeating the same operation, declared 'More than a hundred years!' Kalicharan was finally convinced.

For Kelucharan, it was not difficult to differentiate a new *pothi* from an old one. In the villages the elders carried old illustrated manuscripts to be read by the pundits during certain festivals and he, as a child, used to toddle around, immensely attracted by the colourful illustrations in them. Many a times he had seen the elders performing this type of test in order to determine the approximate age of manuscripts.

The Odissi renderings of Jayadeva's poems, presented by Kumkum during the seminar, were appreciated for their lyrical grace and subtlety of expression. Besides the two new compositions, her performance included, '*lalita labanga lata-parishilana*' (an earlier composition that was completed with additional music portions for the occasion) and '*pashyati dishi dishi*'. 'Little Padmavati', as Kumkum was called by the other participants at the seminar, had absorbed the best in *abhinaya* from both her gurus, Mayadhar and Kelucharan; this, along with her childlike and versatile face, lent a quality of spontaneity to her *abhinaya* which went very well with the natural grace of the Odissi style.

In spite of the success of the presentation, the next day a daily newspaper carried some adverse comments by Rukmini Devi Arundale, who apparently was present during the Odissi demonstration and had left the hall soon after. The comments were on the 'vulgarity' of the items

presented and her opinion that such explicit allusions of an erotic nature should not be portrayed in dance.

Reacting to this, Suresh Awasthi, Secretary of the Sangeet Natak Akademi, the next day requested Kelucharan to interpret some of the *ashtapadis* in front of an invited audience; Kelucharan demonstrated five stanzas of the *Dashavatara* and at the request of those present, he performed the *ashtapadi 'dhira samire'*. This was perhaps his first public demonstration of the *Gita Govinda* outside Orissa. Rukmini Devi was not present at this performance.

A few years later, in February 1968, when Sonal Mansingh, who had started learning Odissi from Kelucharan since 1965, was invited to give a series of performances by some of the *sabhas* in Madras, Rukmini Devi witnessed the first of the performances at the Museum Theatre. On this occasion Sonal performed the last song of the poem '*Kuru Yadunandana chandanasisiratarena karena payodhare*' (Yadava hero, your hand is cooler than the sandalbalm on my breast), which had been composed with her in Cuttack. The song is perhaps one of the most erotic as far as the meaning is concerned: Radha, after her union with Krishna, requests her lover to decorate her breasts with sandalwood paste, apply *kajal* to her eyes, put in order her ruffled hair and cover her naked loins with ornaments. Rukmini Devi was finally won over; not only did she not see any 'vulgarity' in the dance composition but was also full of praise for both the dancer and the guru.

She found the interpretation totally faithful to the lyric and highly aesthetic. The following day the newspapers reported Rukmini's fulsome praise for the artists, and this brought a lot of favourable publicity for the Odissi dance form.

In December of the next year, in 1969 Sonal was invited to perform at the Music Academy and, at the request of Y.G. Doraiswamy, an eminent organizer of dance programmes in Madras, Kelucharan gave a demonstration the same morning. The hall was packed. Kelucharan danced for about one and a half hour only with vocal accompaniment. After demonstrating the basic steps and *bhangis* he danced *'pashyati dishi dishi'*. Sonal had simultaneously begun explaining his dance in English but was interrupted; Kelucharan's *abhinaya* was self-explanatory and did not need any further interpretation. He remembers how, after finishing the performance, three women had come to him

Kelucharan giving demonstration at the Seminar on Gita Govinda *organized by the Sangeet Natak Akademi in Delhi, 1967 (facing page).*

and placing their hands over his head, told him in Tamil: 'Tonight we had a *darshana* of Lord Jagannath through your dance. May the Lord bless you!'

The evening performance by Sonal was a triumph. At the end of it, eminent Bharatanatyam Guru Ramiah Pillai approached Kelucharan from behind, while he was still sitting on the stage, and literally raised him in the air, exclaiming: 'What a unique way of accompanying on the pakhawaj!'

In spite of these successes it took some more years before Odissi training was finally accepted in the precincts of the Kalakshetra, Rukmini Devi's sacred temple of Bharatanatyam teaching. This happened only after the successful *arengetram* (first stage performance) of some of the Madras based dancers, trained both by Kelucharan and Ramani Ranjan Jena. Among them were Mirtha, Rani Sunanda, Meria, Padma Sukumar, Alarmel Valli and Malavika Sarukkhai. It was in fact only around 1978 that Ramani was asked by Rukmini Devi to occupy a bungalow in one corner of the Kalakshetra compound for his classes. By this time Ramani had already been in Madras for four to five years and had managed to give training individually to the dancers, some of whom had started learning during the Kala Vikash Kendra summer courses.

When Kelucharan started composing the '*Kuru Yadunandana*' song for Sonal, her father-in-law, Mayadhar Mansingh, had some reservations and called on him to say that he did not think it appropriate for a lady of a respectable family to portray a song in which the heroine was depicted as being naked.[2]

Kelucharan asked him to see the rehearsal first, and then, if he was still of the same opinion, he would stop teaching. After seeing the composition of the first stanza, Mansingh's doubts were dispelled; he recognized the aesthetic beauty, the respect for the lyric and above all the underlying devotional approach which removed any trace of vulgarity from the interpretation.

While teaching this dance piece during the summer workshops Kelucharan would talk to the students who were married (including the ones coming from outside India even if unmarried) and explain to them the subtle meaning of the *abhinaya*. The younger students would be asked to just copy his movements.

The exquisite sitting postures envisaged for Radha in the

[2] This is the version told to me by Guruji. According to Sonal it was Dr. Mansingh who convinced the hesitant and shy Kelucharan to take up this song.

Kelucharan in his famous portrayal of Radha from the concluding song of the Gita Govinda 'Kuru Yadunandana'.

'*Kuru Yadunandana*' composition had been meticulously sketched by Kelucharan during his visits to the Konarka Temple in the early fifties, i.e. the period between his leaving the Annapurna A Group and joining the Kala Vikash Kendra. It had been his mother who had first explained to him the beautiful poses of the sculptures of the Sun Temple and since then he had often dreamt about them.

He could visualize the same postures while Kumkum's mother sat on the floor cutting the *gua* (areca nut) for preparing *pan* or making sandalwood paste for the worship of the deity. He would often point out to Kumkum the graceful way she would sit watching the rehearsals of the composition: she would curl her knee near her chest with a slight inclination of the hip and her head resting on her raised knee.

Kelucharan drew his inspiration from all that was happening around him; the swaying movement of the hips of a woman passing by on the road or the heaving of the chest by another while walking would be transformed into graceful *hansa gati* (swan gait) and *mayura gati* (peacock gait) in his compositions. It were the common place actions that would provide him with material for fresh inputs into his dance. His fertile imagination would not miss a single message coming from any source and use it to enrich his dance vocabulary. His dance movements would be inspired by vendors in the marketplace, the boatmen rowing on the lake, snake charmers at the village fairs or workers carrying loads on their back. The world of women held a special place in Kelucharan's fertile imagination: their feelings, reactions, body language and personalities provided him with inexhaustible material to be transformed into the exquisite language of his *abhinaya*.

In Kelucharan's own words:

> What is important is to observe and absorb the way women do their chores. It has to go straight into the blood, and while reproducing it a great artist always adds something of his own. Radha' s character in the different songs of the *Gita Govinda*, has gradually matured over the years. For me the proximity with women is essential to be able to absorb as much as possible their characteristics. Once somebody, whose sister was learning from me, passed this comment 'How lucky Kelucharan is! To be always among women!' I asked him 'Is not your sister among my students?' He was left speechless and immediately apologized.

After receiving the Sangeet Natak Akademi Award, Kelucharan had the option of getting a grant from the Akademi and start teaching on his own. He suggested instead that the grant be given to the Kala Vikash Kendra to enable it to start special short-term advanced training courses during summer. His idea was to condense the training sessions to a period of two to three months so that for the rest of the year he could travel all over India and impart training to students of Odissi residing outside the state. For the same reason he had also turned down the offer to teach at the Sangeet Mahavidyalay at Bhubaneswar, and instead suggested Pankaj Charan's name for the post.

The 'summer courses', as these training sessions were called, were started at the Kala Vikash Kendra in 1968 and continued for five to six years. The duration of the courses was three months at a time, with classes being held all day long. The Akademi grant for holding such condensed courses was between Rs. 5,000 to 10,000 per year; Kelucharan's stipend was kept at Rs. 900 for three months, while the rest of the money was utilized towards providing stipends to students (Rs. 75 each), expenditure on the construction of a hall, etc.

To popularize the courses, some of the male students who had just completed their training at the Sangeet Mahavidyalay, were included in the first batch. Besides them, among the first female students were Sonal, Aparajita, Kunkumina, Ratna, Nandita Samuel, Swadhina Bose, Parvin, Nasrim, Rani Karnaa, Snehaprava and Menaka Thakker. Some of them stayed in the hostel at the Kala Vikash Kendra, while others would found their own accommodation elsewhere. It was only in the mid seventies that the students began residing at Kelucharan's house.

The summer courses soon attracted dancers from outside the state. One of the first to attend them was Menaka Thakker who, after seeing the Odissi dance-drama *Krishna Leela* in Bombay in December 1964 by the Kala Vikash Kendra troupe, had immediately asked Babulal Doshi to send an Odissi teacher to Bombay. Kelucharan could not be sent at the time because of his illness, so it fell to one of his senior students, Ramani Ranjan Jena to take up the assignment. Ramani stayed in Menaka's house for about a year and taught her all the rudiments of the style. When he was called back to Cuttack to substitute for Kelucharan as a regular teacher at the Kala Vikash Kendra, Menaka then started going to Orissa. The first time she went there, the summer courses had not yet started, so she stayed in a small room near the entrance of the Kendra. Kelucharan used to teach her here. The first night though, after her arrival, she was at the hospital attending to Laxmipriya who had just had a miscarriage; Kelucharan was not allowed in the female ward and other than her nobody else was around to help out.

In the summer of 1967 Rani Karnaa joined Kelucharan's classes. However, by then she had already received extensive training in Bharatanatyam and Kathak.

'I had seen Priyambada's performance in Delhi during the 3rd Inter University Youth Festival in 1956 and I was totally taken by the beauty of the Odissi style', she remembers, and adds:

> but it was only in 1967, when, after my marriage, I came to Cuttack as an Oriya 'bohu' (wife) that I could get in touch with Kelu Babu. He was very happy to take me on as his student not only because I had already been trained in two classical styles, but above all because I had become an Oriya 'bohu'. He used to call me

'Nua Bohu' (new wife). My son was already 4 years old by that time; he was of the same age as Ratikanta, Kelu Babu's son. Since I had already been trained for one year by Hari Krishna Behera in Delhi before joining Kelu Babu, I was able to give my first performance of Odissi at Sapru House in October 1967. On that occasion I presented two *pallavi* in Raga Shankara Bharana and Kalyani, besides *mangala charan*, *batu* and *Dashavatara*. It was quite a heavy repertoire and I was feeling extremely nervous. I was actually petrified with fear and almost unable to step onto the stage. Kelu Babu did all what he could at reassuring me and giving me confidence. I will never forget all the patience, love and affection which he showered on me that day.

Among the students to join the summer course in the late sixties was Myrta Barvie from Argentina, perhaps the first of Kelucharan's 'foreign' student. She had already completed a five year course of Bharatanatyam at Kalakshetra, Madras, when she happened to see an Odissi dance performance by one of Kelucharan's disciple in Delhi. Overwhelmed by the beauty of the dance and the music, she straightway asked Kelucharan to be accepted as his student and since then has studied with him in Orissa and New Delhi.

In 1970, the summer course was joined by a batch of girls from Delhi: Darshana, Veena, Nalini and Kumkum Lal. They had all begun learning Odissi in Delhi at the Nritya Niketan, started in 1965 by Hari Krishna Behera, who had shifted to Delhi after completing the six year course at the Kala Vikash Kendra. Initially the classes were held at the residence of Shri Badrinath Khosla, who had a spacious house in Bhagat Singh Market and whose daughter and niece were students of Hari Krishna.

A native of Balasore in northern Orissa, Hari Krishna had come to Delhi in 1964 on an Orissa government scholarship of Rs. 75 per month to study Kathak dance from Birju Maharaj. His real dream though was to be able to promote Odissi in the capital, and soon he had his first set of private students. He had struggled hard to complete the dance course at the Kendra; he had come to Cuttack for the certificate which could not be obtained from the Nrutya Sangeet Kala Mandir at Balasore, where he had had his initial training in dance. He was practically penniless and Kelucharan had provided considerable assistance to him during those years. A meticulous and hard working student, Hari Krishna was the only one perhaps at that time who would write down in detail all the compositions that he had learnt. He also wrote the entire *Abhinaya Darpana* in Oriya script so that Kelucharan could read it.

Hara Kirshna Behera and Ramani Ranjan Jena, also from Balasore district, were among the few male students who regularly attended the classes at the Kala Vikash Kendra during the early sixties. The general opinion was that, no matter how much talent a male Odissi dancer may have, it would hardly be possible for him to pursue the career of a performing artist.

With the predominance of the *lasya* element in this style there is hardly any scope for the male body to fulfil its potential. Public opinion, which all these years was totally against women performing this dance, had taken an about turn and now very much preferred female dancers on the stage.

Male dancers could at best become good teachers or enact male roles in dance-drama compositions, but to sustain a regular Odissi performance all on their own was almost unthinkable. Ramani remembers that to stick to his decision of becoming a performing artist, how much struggle he

Kelucharan in Delhi in the early 1970s, sitting between Sanjukta on his left and Birju Maharaj on his right. Behind them are three of his male students: Surendra Nath Jena, Ramani Ranjan Jena and Hari Krishna Behera.

had to wage against the general advice, including that of men like Dhirendranath Pattanayak and Bhubaneswar Mishra. At one stage the proposal by Ram Gopal Mishra, the Kathak master who used to visit the Kala Vikash Kendra, that he give up the Odissi style and follow him to Lucknow to practice the Kathak style seemed the most likely solution to his dilemma.

At that point it was Kelucharan who convinced him not to abandon his art, and the advice bore fruit when finally in 1963 Ramani was able to give his first solo performance on stage at Bhadrak. Kelucharan accompanied him on the pakhawaj with only a vocalist as a second accompanist. His repertoire was almost standard at that time, it included *Nomami Vignaraja* (Salutation to the remover of obstacles) as *mangala charan*, *pallavi* in Raga Kalyani, '*lalita labanga lata*', and a small *mokshia* at the end. He had to design his costume and ornaments on that occasion, since everything until then had been crafted for the female dancer.

It was an important event not only for Ramani, who had finally fulfilled his dream, but also for the future male dancers. Ramani went a long way after that first performance, both as a teacher and performer. In the late seventies, he perhaps reached the climax of his career as a dancer, by appearing regularly on stage, both in India and abroad, with his star pupil Malavika Sarukkhai.

In 1968 Kelucharan spent three months at a stretch at the Nritya Niketan, after Mayadhar Rout left having taught there for a couple of years. It was while Kelucharan was teaching at this school that the Delhi based dancer Yamini Krishnamuthy, by then an already established Bharatanatyam and Kuchipudi exponent, started learning from him.

'Yamini was a very temperamental but sincere student', recalls Kelucharan, and narrates an incident:

I was once teaching her in her father's house the *ashtapadi* '*Kuru Yadunandana*' and she got stuck at the line '*mama rucire cikure Kuru manada*' (put flowers in my shining hair loosened by loveplay, oh Krishna). I demonstrated that same line several times, but she was still not able to get the right flow in her execution. Her father, who was watching the scene, pointed this out to her, and she got so upset that she ran to the kitchen and started throwing down glasses and plates. Her sister explained to me what was happening. I assured them that she would finally be able to learn. Besides receiving lessons at home, Yamini also started coming to the Kala Niketan. When she presented the same item on the stage in Delhi, she was able to perform it with the right degree of smoothness and restraint. However, I could not be present for her second programme at Madras. She insisted on being accompanied by her *mridanga* player. After a few days she met me in Bombay and with tears in her eyes she showed me the adverse comments which came out in the newspapers about her performance. She told me that she would not dance Odissi any more if I did not accompany her. I had no more occasion to play for her after that.

In October 1969 Kelucharan gave his second lecture demonstration in the capital, this time at the National Museum Auditorium. The function was organized by Badrinath Khosla, with the help of Rani Karnaa and Dr S.K. Saxena, who also compered the programme. Besides demonstrating the technical vocabulary of Odissi Kelucharan rendered the *ashtapadi* '*pashyati dishi dishi*'.

Mohan Khokar in his review of the lecture demonstration observed: 'One could not but marvel at the extraordinary control he [Kelucharan] has over his body. . . . He has not only a strong technique but also a very intelligent and sensitive approach to it. In "*pashyati dishi dishi*". . . his eloquence at times was not merely touching but heart-wringing.'[3]

In January 1970, along with the students of the Nrutya Niketan, Kelucharan choreographed the Odissi dance-drama *Kanchi Vijaya* (Victory over Kanchi), which was presented at the Fine Arts Theatre on Rafi Marg. Rani Karnaa was in the role of Manika, the milk seller, Hari Krishna Behera was the Gajapati king, Kumkum Lal portrayed Lord Jagannath and Sonal Mansingh was Padmavati while Veena, Nalini and Darshana were the *maharis*.

While in Delhi Kelucharan would spend two to three months either at Khosla's house or at the residence of one of his students. His collaboration with the Nrutya Niketan lasted until 1971, the year in which the school was closed down. Khosla's daughter, after marriage, had gone abroad and his niece had started acting in films. As a result Khosla lost interest in running the school. In November of the same year Kumkum Lal had her *mancha pravesh* in Delhi.

Before this event Kelucharan had spent three months at Kumkum's residence behind the Kamani Hall near Mandi House. During his stay, the other students, Nalini, Sonal, etc., would join the classes conducted in the house.

[3] *Hindustan Times*, New Delhi, 6 October 1969.

Kumkum's dance programme at the AIFACS Hall included, besides the *mangala charan* and the *pallavi* in the Ragas Shankara Bharanam and Saveri, the two *abhinaya* compositions '*yahi Madhava yahi Kesava*' and '*Bibhushana puspe*', both in their complete versions.

The two *pallavis* in Ragâs Shankara Bharanam and Saveri had been composed in the years 1965 and 1967 respectively at Kumkum Das' house in Cuttack, where Kelucharan, Bhubaneswar Mishra and the singer Rakhal Mohanty, would get together for days and work out the details and nuances of the composition in perfect unison of mind and inspiration. Kelucharan provided the rhythmic structure, Bhubaneswar Mishra the melodious tune woven around the '*tari jam*' phrase and Rakhal Mohanty the vocal support. To date these two *pallavi* compositions have remained the most widely performed by generations of Odissi dancers; they have been handed down from 'guru' to 'guru' and have become a reference point for the *nritta* (pure dance) compositions.

A third *pallavi* which became equally popular was the one in Raga Arabi, commonly known also as '*re re pa ma*'

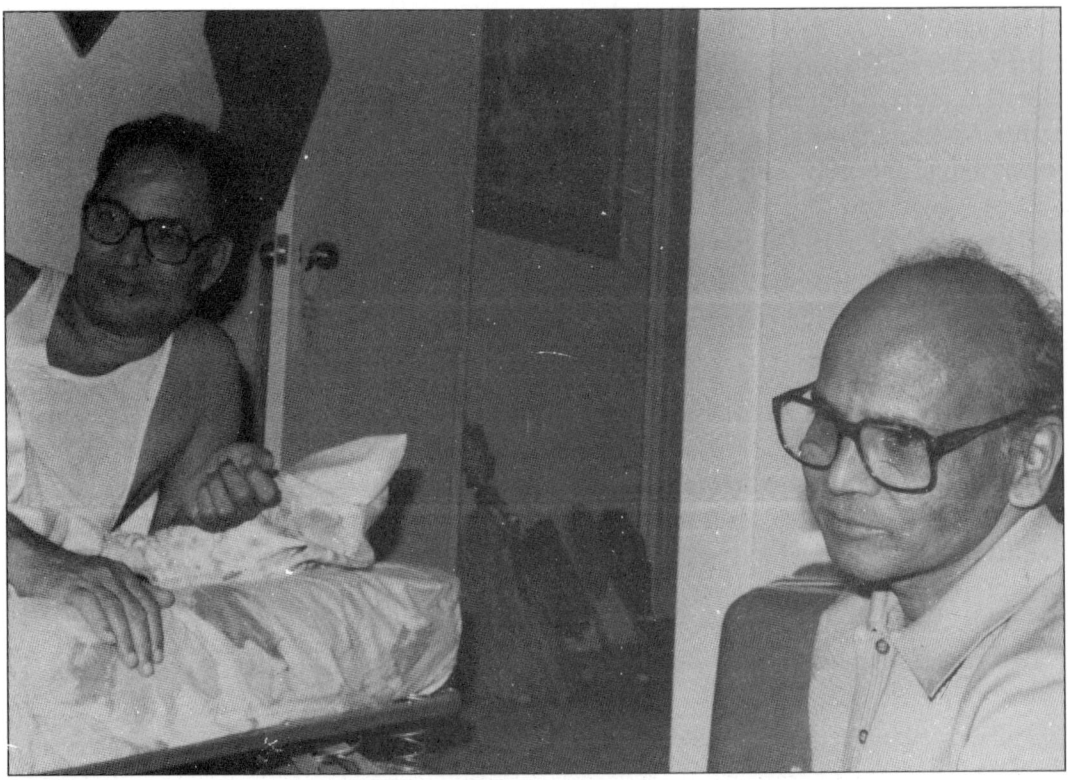

Kelucharan with Bhubaneswar Mishra in a relaxed mood.

because of the *swara* (notes) sung by the singer all along the composition. Work on this composition was started by Kelucharan in 1968 but due to his two and half months tour of Russia with Sonal that year and the subsequent absence of Kumkum, who had joined the training academy in Mussorie, it could only be completed on her return in 1971. For a short period during Kelucharan's absence, Pankaj Charan had been called in by Kumkum's father to teach her; it was during this period that some of the 'wave' type movements of the torso ('you should feel as if you are wiping a glass window with a soft cloth' Kelucharan would say while teaching it) which characterize this *pallavi* had been envisaged. On resuming the work Kelucharan was able to elaborate these movements and to create around them a well-knit and harmonic composition where melody, rhythm and choreography merged in perfect unison. This *pallavi* took its final shape with Kumkum Lal's performance in 1972 and from then on it has been handed down without any major changes.

During the Dussehra vacation in 1971 the duo Kelucharan and Bhubaneswar Mishra composed another *pallavi* in the Raga Bageshree, called '*gatibheda pallavi*'. It was to be performed by Kumkum Das in Delhi in December of the same year. To date this *pallavi* remains the most complicated and structurally perfect among Kelucharan's *nritta* compositions, where all the five variations of *gati* (equally distributed divisions of the time cycle) have been utilized.

This *pallavi* was performed by Kumkum Das in a *jugalbandi* with Roshan Kumari during a performance at the Birla Matushri Hall in Bombay in 1972; the pattern of the *pallavi* was such that it offered the Kathak dancer ample scope for improvization while allowing both the styles to maintain their own distinct characteristics.

This group of *pallavi*, along with a few others composed in later years in the Ragas Khamaj and Hamsadhwani (1979), Belahari (1983), Kirwani (1981) and Bihag (1988), represent the most fruitful phase of collaboration between the duo Kelucharan and Bhubaneswar Mishra; there was a sort of 'magical' understanding between them, so that each was able to anticipate and give expression to the other's expectations without having to discuss it. After Mishraji's death in 1993, Kelucharan has still not been able to find a substitute for him; his 'pure dance' compositions of the later years lack that harmonious blend of melody and rhythm of the previous ones and inevitably had a virtuosic quality, with the rhythmic elaborations prevailing over the melodic ones.

Unfortunately, by the end of the sixties, jealousy, frustration and possessiveness had crept into the world of Odissi dance form. The years of the Jayantika resolutions seemed far away and personal gains and ambitions had started creating scars and resentments. Mayadhar left Orissa frustrated at not receiving, according to him, due recognition and credit for his contributions and indirectly accusing Kelucharan for having deprived him 'not only of my students but also smothered the fertility of my mind',[4] while Hari Krishna Behera felt deceived by Kelucharan when he forbade Kumkum Lal to teach him the *arabhi pallavi*.

It all started when, on his return from the village, Hari Krishna found that Khosla had closed down the school. He was suddenly without a job and by now most of his ex-students had switched over to Kelucharan. It was at this point that a misunderstanding arose about the *arabi pallavi*; Kelucharan forbade Kumkum from teaching Hari Krishna as he wanted the latter to come and learn it directly from him. But Hari Krishna took it otherwise. In the same year, Hari Krishna got a teaching assignment in the Gandharva Mahavidyalay, where Madhavi Mudgal started learning Odissi from him. When finally in 1974 Madhavi also left him, although she did so only after having sought his permission, for continuing her training with Kelucharan, his resentment grew still further and unfortunately never abated.

A similar situation arose when Kelucharan started teaching at the Triveni Kala Sangam, between 1974 and 1976. He would stay in Delhi for about two months in the school premises. During this period, students being taught by Mayadhar and Surendra Nath Jena would come to Kelucharan to learn from him. When Kelucharan became aware of the complaints from these gurus he told Mrs Shridharani, the director of the school, not to admit new students unless they produced written permission from their teachers. This problem could not be resolved easily; it continued to resurface more or less all through Kelucharan's career. While some of the younger teachers accepted the fact and saw it as a natural phenomenon, others could not

[4] Jayantika souvenir, New Delhi, 1985.

come to terms with the reality and cut themselves off from him.

Many of the students who joined Kelucharan's classes at Triveni were already acquainted with the other styles of dance such as Manipuri (Charu Singh and Sharon Lowen), Bharatanatyam (Jayalaxmi and Myrta Barvie), Mohinyattam (Bharati Shivaji), Kathak (Madhavi Mudgal and Rani Karnaa) and modern dance (Sheila Raj).

Madhavi Mudgal had met Kelucharan in Bombay in 1972 by sheer accident. She had gone there to give a performance scheduled at the Bhulabhai Memorial Institute when she suddenly found that she did not have a pakhawaj player because Hari Krishna could not reach there from Delhi on time. Bhubaneswar Mishra, who was working with the All India Radio in Bombay at that time and was supposed to play for Madhavi, informed her that Kelucharan was in town and that she could use his services. Contacted at the last moment, Kelucharan went directly on the stage to play without any rehearsal.

Later, in 1975, Madhavi played the role of Krishna, in the Hindi version of the *Gita Govinda,* a ballet produced in Bombay by the Pundit Mothiram Sangeet Natya Academy with music by Pundit Jasraj. Among others in the cast were Tejashree, Jaya Dheer and Protima Bedi. The ballet troupe travelled extensively and contributed a great deal towards popularizing Odissi in this region.

Kelucharan's classes in Bombay were first held in the school of Jogendra Desai at Chowpatty, then called the Sanskruti Bhawan. It is here that he coined the famous refrain which he would sing before handing over the cassettes with the dance music to the students at the conclusion of any workshop: '*Layahe cassette, Chowpatty jaunga, bhelpuri khaunga, nachunga Basanta pallavi, ta kita jham, tari kita jham.*'

He shifted the classes for a couple of years to Jaya Dheer's house, and later on was associated with the Odissi Institute opened at Juhu by Protima Bedi and with the Soli Batliwalla Institute on Warden Road. Finally, from 1981 onwards he started holding a month long workshop twice a year at the National Centre for the Performing Arts at Nariman Point. Most of his students from Bombay—Jhelum, Devi, Uma, Hema, Minal, started learning during this period. Some of them joined him after having learnt

the preliminary steps from other teachers like Shankar Behera and Natabhar Maharana who had already settled down in Bombay.

By the mid seventies Kelucharan had completed the construction of the dance hall in his house and was not only able to teach a larger number of students but also to provide accommodation for them during the training period. For this purpose a new room had been constructed on top of the storeroom, after converting the thatched roof into a concrete one. Even before the construction of this room, some of the male students like Giridhari, Kishore, Linga, Murali, Shamir, at times would stay the night in Charu's room while the female students had to find accommodation outside the house, either with relatives or in the Kala Vikash Kendra guest room. Once the extra room was ready and the outstation female dancers were accommodated in the house, the male students were not allowed to stay in the house during the night.

Kelucharan used to be very firm on this issue. Odissi dance had just emerged from a dark period of degeneration, and public opinion had finally turned favourable towards it leaving behind all previous doubts and suspicions.

Girls from educated families had come forward to learn the dance and Kelucharan felt that their reputation must not be sullied. When Sonal Mansingh decided to leave her husband, Kelucharan's reaction was adamant; she was not accepted as his student any more, lest people should begin to think that Odissi and family life were incompatible. At that point of time, with few exceptions, Oriya girls, once married, were rarely seen in the class any more. It was painful enough for him to have to lose a dancer every time any of his good students married. He, therefore, did not want Sonal's case to further aggravate the situation.

When Protima Bedi landed in Cuttack in the mid seventies to learn Odissi from him, she was immediately asked to give up jeans and cigarettes and change her free lifestyle at least during the training period. It is true that, with the passage of time, Kelucharan became more tolerant and less interfering in the private lives of his students, adjusting to the changing times, but at least for the first two decades after the revival of the dance, he was very strict.

Even though he became considerably tolerant, Kelucharan still advised his married students to adopt an attitude of compromise in case of a family crisis, advising

Kelucharan with Protima Bedi on his right and Jaya Dheer on his left during the rehearsals for the Gita Govinda *ballet, 1975 (facing page).*

Laxmipriya.

them against taking rash decisions. Besides he even tried to mediate between quarelling partners and pacify them whenever possible. When Sanjukta and her husband Raghunath, a renowned vocalist whom she had married during her stay in Madras, had remained separated for almost a year Kelucharan succeded in bringing them back together with a solemn promise in front of Lord Jagannath that they will never leave each other again.

Sutapa Duttagupta, his Bengali student, remembers how, in the early nineties, while Kelucharan was staying at her house to rehearse for a performance, her husband as a result of a minor quarrel with her threatened not to attend the performance. On hearing this with tears in his eyes, Kelucharan pleaded with the husband and refused to play if he did not attend the show. Not only did Kelucharan make him promise that he would attend the show but till the curtains went up kept on enquiring if he had arrived and relaxed only after being assured that the husband was sitting in the front row of the auditorium.

Kelucharan displays the same attitude towards his own family—always careful not to neglect the slightest change of mood in Laxmipriya's behaviour; a raised voice coming from the other room is enough to make him rise to his feet, interrupting whatever work he may be doing. Until and unless the problem is sorted out he cannot concentrate on his work. To him peace in the family always comes first no matter what. Greatly concerned for his wife, he tries to satisfy all her whims and wishes. He leaves the responsibilities of the entire household on her, without arguing or entering into a discussion. It is moving to watch how protective he becomes towards her especially while travelling by train: he will prepare her bed, help her lie down and sit on the edge of her berth until she falls asleep so as to shield her from possible disturbances from other passengers.

He needs to have her sitting near him at the start of any creative work and she is always the first one in front of whom Kelucharan would present a new work. Many of us who have been his student often say that Guruma must be reaping the fruits of a positive *karma* in her previous life for having found such a loving and dedicated husband during this one!

By now Kelucharan's dream had come true; he was able to travel as much as he liked and spread the dance form at all the major centres and, during summer months, he could concentrate on giving training to students in his own home. His own lifestyle was perfectly in tune with this style of functioning; it would have been impossible for him to regulate his way of teaching to an hourly basis or a fixed period of time.

Training sessions could only be regulated by the intensity of the work and not by the hour of the clock. Kelucharan's involvement in his work is so intense that days and nights merge and become a single entity. As a result he only becomes aware of the passage of time if somebody else is there to remind him. Avinash Pasricha during one of his photographic tours of Orissa, was visiting Kelucharan's house during the course of one of the summer workshops. He remembers how Kelucharan went on and on teaching the same line of an *ashtapadi* because the girls were not able to understand it. At last he said: 'We will stop here for today because I have a guest and I have to offer dinner to him.' It was past midnight!

The only activity which was performed at the appointed time was the evening *arati* to the deities, when Kelucharan invariably played the gong surrounded by all the students; this was followed by the singing of *bhajans* and recitation of prayers.

Because of his constant movement from place to place,

Kelucharan performing arati *in front of the shrine at his Cuttack residence.*

people started calling him the 'jet set guru' and he was accused of having inaugurated the age of 'quick formula'. His detractors would say that by attending a few workshops one could learn the required number of dance pieces for a public performance. In reality there was never any compromise on his part; on the contrary his teaching has become increasingly meticulous and rigorous with the passage of time. But much depends on the students themselves, their commitment to the dance to enable them to keep practicing even when they are on their own.

While enriching his experience through a wider exposure, Kelucharan kept on working on the minor details of the style by constantly redefining the basic texture of the movements. And questions posed by dancers, who have been exposed to other dance styles, stimulated him towards finding still greater precision in his approach.

By now the synchronization between the footwork and the beats of the pakhawaj had become much more accurate than what it was to begin with, and the definition of the movements of the upper torso both in the *tribhanga* and *chowka* position had emerged in a clearer way. The precision of the torso movements became in course of the years Kelucharan's 'stamp' in the various Odissi *gharanas*. He kept elaborating this detail until his style reached its full maturity in the early eighties.

Although the deflection of the upper torso is very much a part of the *tribhanga* posture and is also present in the *gotipua* style, it was only Kelucharan who stretched this movement to the extreme, adding gracefulness and lightness to each posture. The swinging of the torso and steadiness of the hips are among the major contributions of Kelucharan towards evolving a classical style of Odissi.

The basic steps which until the mid sixties were only six, with three to four variants for each step, by now had become ten for each *tribhanga* and *chowka* position and the footwork and basic positions of the feet had become more defined and articulate. The *batu* too had acquired a more precise structure and was altogether more complex than what it used to be during the time of the Jayantika.

Kelucharan came back from Delhi in the early seventies with a brand new moped, a Viky, which he had bought with the money received from Khosla after the *Kanchi Vijaya* ballet, the contributions from students and from his own earnings. He used to move around very proudly on his brand new Viky with his dhoti flying. By this time he had almost stopped giving private tuitions, and the local students during their summer holidays joined the classes at the Kala Vikash Kendra.

Among the Oriya students who joined the summer courses in the early seventies were Nandita Pattanayak, Sikata Das, Sabita Sahu, Sarita Mohapatra, Preeti Mohapatra, Itishree Panda, Pranati Parija, Prabhati Panda and Giridhari Nayak. Among them Nandita, Giridhari, Pranati and Itishree got Central Goverment scholarships for advance training from Kelucharan, and continued to learn at his house even after he discontinued the summer courses at the Kala Vikash Kendra.

During these years some of the dance-dramas which had been composed in the sixties, like the *Gita Govinda*, *Shakuntala*, *Konarka* and *Kanchi Vijaya* were revived by Kelucharan for performing on the occasion of science and medical conferences organized at the S.C.B. Medical College in Cuttack. Dr Ananga Dwibedi, an anaesthestist with a keen interest in the performing arts, was mainly responsible for the organization of such events.

Kelucharan in the role of the chief sculptor Bishu Maharana in ballet Konarka *(Cuttack, 1975).*

In the dance-drama *Konarka*, staged in 1975 for the All-India Conference on Pathology and Microbiology, the doctor was supposed to play the role of Bishu Maharana, the chief sculptor under whose direction the entire temple was to be constructed, but he backed out one week before the show expressing his inability to do the role. Kelucharan had no other option but to take up the role himself, something which he continued to do in the subsequent rendition of the same production. After his inspiring interpretation nobody else could ever have played that role again with such a finesse! Among the other roles that he played during this period included the king of Kanchi in the dance-drama *Kanchi Vijaya* and that of Jayadeva in the *Gita Govinda* ballet.

Kumkum Das had given her last performace in February 1972 in Calcutta and then, for about ten years after her marriage, she stopped performing, while Sanjukta, in spite of her family life and two kids, appeared on stage more and more frequently. Two major dance pieces that were composed for her in the seventies were the *Sita Harana* episode from Tulsidas' *Sri Ramcharitmanas*, composed in 1973 for the Tulsidas Chatusata Samaroha in Delhi, and *Ardhanariswar* based on the Shankaracharya text composed in 1977. By now Kelucharan was no longer free to accompany her on all the performances and Bonomali Maharana, Kelucharan's cousin (brother), took his place.

Though Kelucharan has taught hundreds of students over the years, it was with Kumkum and Sanjukta that his relationship was the most paternal and affectionate. Although very different from each other, the first naughty and jovial and the second serious and professional, Kelucharan nevertheless chose to pair them as male and female characters in many of his dance-dramas. He had seen them growing from the tender age of five and considered them a part of his family.

It was on Kumkum that, in the mid-sixties, he had hand-stitched the first Odissi dance costume using her father's old dhoti. All this was done in front of a stunned Bhagirathi, who would later become the 'official' tailor of all the Odissi dancers. Kelucharan had dressed many a dancer during the Kala Vikash Kendra period, when the stitched sari had not yet been introduced and each of the participants had to be draped in a four and a half yard sari so that he was now able to visualize quite easily which portion of the sari should be used for which part of the costume. Bhagirathi was at that time Kumkum's family tailor and hardly knew that, his meeting with Kelucharan, would change his entire life. Although it took him some years and quite a lot of scolding to learn after that first lesson, he finally developed the skill and started earning his bread by producing Odissi costumes exclusively.

While Kumkum had the privilege to wear the first stitched dress on the stage, Sanjukta was the one to wear a *benga patia* (silver belt) for the first time during the All-India Dance Seminar in Hyderabad in 1963. In the *Abhinaya Chandrika* written by Maheswara Mohapatra, there is a mention of an ornament called *bega mukha* (frog head) to be worn around the waist but nobody until then had been able to find out what it looked like. One day Dhirendranath Pattanayak hit upon the idea of asking one Harihar Khuntia, a Brahmin from Puri who was scheduled to come to Bhubaneswar to teach Odissi at the Kala Kendra, to bring with him the *pedi* (secret box made out of bamboo where all the family ornaments were kept) belonging to his mother. Inside it, among other jewels, he found a silver *benga patia*, all blackened and broken. He thought it may be the same belt which was mentioned in the *Abhinaya Chandrika* as *bega mukha.* He decided to give some money to Harihar Kuntia's mother, and borrow it from her. It was the day before the departure of Sanjukta and Mayadhar for Hyderabad where both were to dance accompanied by Kelucharan on the pakhawaj. At the same function Dhirendranath Pattanayak was to read a paper on the *karana* (sets of movements) used in Odissi. During the train journey Kelucharan re-threaded the belt and after reaching Hyderabad, bought a kilogram of tamarind and cleaned the *benga patia*. That evening Sanjukta for the first time wore the ornament, which perhaps more than any other is regarded as the hallmark of the Odissi costume.

While Sanjukta soon became quite independent in her dance, Kumkum continued to depend on Kelucharan even after resuming her dance in the early eighties. He always did her make-up for each performance, tied her ankle bells and played the pakhawaj for her. While all other students, after the construction of the dance hall, came to Kelucharan's home to learn, Kumkum was the only one to receive Kelucharan's dance lessons in her own house at least till 1984, the year in which she started the Odissi Research

Centre in Bhubaneswar, and had Kelucharan as the main 'architect' for about ten years.

Sanjukta remained faithful to her guru all through, no matter how famous and important she had become over the years. One call from him was enough to make her drop everything and be at his disposal. She always remained till the end the most talented and receptive among his students, the one with whom he enjoyed composing, for he valued her memory, precision and her outstanding grasp of rhythm. Both of them would be busy composing late in the night without ever being tired; he would keep on trying new combinations of steps and with equal verstality she would reproduce each variant.

It was often dawn before she would return to Bhubaneswar after working the whole night and still she would never complain or show any sign of fatigue. On the contrary the next day she would try to reach a little earlier so as to be able to join the classes with all of us. At the news of her premature death in June 1997, Kelucharan was left shattered for days together refusing to believe that his 'daughter' had departed before him. 'I cannot create another Sanjukta', he declared after her death, confirming that she was unique in many ways.

It was with her that Kelucharan made his first trip abroad in 1967. They had been sent to Russia by the Indian Government as part of a large delegation of artists, as India's cultural ambassadors. Besided Birju Maharaj and his Kathak group, the troupe included Yamini Krishnamurthy, Gopi Krishna, Bismillah Khan and eminent film artists such as Raj Kapoor, Sunil Dutt and Nargis. The last performance was presented in the Tashkent region with all the artists participating together during a festival which lasted for three consecutive days. It was on the occasion of this trip that Kelucharan's date of birth was set as 1 August 1926. When Sanjukta had to submit his papers to the passport office she realized that his birth certificate was missing so she decided to fix his birthday in the same month as hers. The year was calculated by approximately recounting the major events of his life and finally deciding that it must have been 'around' 1926.

Kelucharan visited the Soviet Union again in 1968 with Sonal, in 1970 with Kumkum Das, and for the Festival of India in Russia in August 1987. Kumkum's mother, who accompanied them during the second tour, remembers how, in spite of not being able to speak a word in any foreign

Kelucharan and Sanjukta on their first trip to Russia in 1967.

language, Kelucharan would make himself understood through drawings. In the restaurant he drew pictures of chicken and pigs to order his food, while in the car he drew Odissi poses and sang '*tari jham*' to the driver to explain his art.

He used to travel with what he called a 'fine art instrument', a basket covered in a silken cloth where he concealed the betel leaves which were not allowed to be taken out of India.

Kelucharan had occasions to improve his English while teaching foreign students, such as Ananda Radha and Sharon Lowen, both from the United States, who joined his classes in the mid seventies, and through his trips abroad. But it always remained a very personalized language, where instead of grammatical rules there were creative and free association of words, gestures and concepts. Although he had barely completed learning the Oriya alphabet during his childhood, in course of time on his own he learnt to recognize the different letters of the English alphabet and was able to read the printed word, while in the spoken medium he conversed freely in Oriya, Bengali and Hindi.

The lack of formal education was amply compensated

in Kelucharan by an amazingly fertile imagination, his ability to observe and his intuitive power combined with an outstanding capacity to be at ease in any circumstance. Every new experience gave him a chance to learn something more; he never tried to conceal or feel shy about his ignorance, and at the same time he never boasted about his achievements. In fact, while dealing with the high-tech world around him Kelucharan continues to be both humble and confident; bowing down and taking up challenges are two attitudes that are not contradictory in his case but coexist in a playful combination.

His practical bent of mind and a sense of curiosity lead him to explore and try out all sorts of mechanical devices, particularly video and audio recording tools.

His association with the movie camera goes back to the mid fifties when for the first time he became the dance director of the Oriya film *Ma*, shot in Calcutta and produced by Gour Ghosh. Laxmipriya was the heroine in the film and Kelucharan performed the folk dance number *Kela Keluni* with two Bengali dancers as his quarrelling wives. This was followed by *Mahalaxmi Puja* produced in 1958 by

A still from a 20-minute documentary film Odissi Dance, *by Ghanashyamo Mohapatra in 1971. Kelucharan is on the pakhawaj while Sanjukta is dancing.*

Krishna Chandra Tripathy, in which Sanjukta and Jayanti did the *Dashavatara* dance. In 1964 he directed a folk dance number, with dances by Mayadhar Rout and Urvashi Joshi, for the film *Manika Jodi* produced by Dhira Biswal, and in 1968 he directed Minati Mishra performing both Odissi and Bharatanatyam pieces for the Oriya film *Arundhati*. During the shooting, film director Tapas Sinha, who happened to be present at the dance rehearsals, asked Kelucharan to direct a dance number for his Bengali film *Nirjana Saikot* (Deserted Beach), for which Minati Mishra rendered the *kalyani pallavi*.

In addition there was an Odissi group dance for the Oriya film *Sudama* produced by Gobind Tej, a *Geeta Natya* composition for the Oriya film *Boitha Bandana* (Puja to the Ship), a folk dance for the film *Ta Poi*; group compositions in Odissi for the film *Sri Krishna Rasa Leela* produced in 1979 by Komal Lochana Mohanty, and an *ashtapadi* from the *Gita Govinda* for the film *Jayadeva*, produced by Sachikanta Rout, with Sharmila Biswas in the role of Padmavati.

During the shooting of these films, Kelucharan did not just give instructions regarding the execution of the choreography but followed every detail concerning camera position, angle, editing process and sound recording.

Kelucharan and Sanjukta dancing together in Switzerland in 1984.

Having accumulated valuable experience he would intervene with his own suggestions and insights.

His expertise especially in the sound editing operations became proverbial over the years to the extent that he was not only able to produce split-second cuts in the dubbing but also could play the pakhawaj and edit the sound at the same time. His first Revox (1/4 inch spool recording machine) was bought during a trip to France with Sanjukta in the early seventies. Until this time he had exercised his editing skill on the tape-recorders available either at the Kala Vikash Kendra or with the students.

All the musical scores of the dance-dramas to be presented at the All-India Medical Conferences held in Cuttack in the late seventies, were recorded late at night in Kelucharan's bedroom. Armed with a single mike, a pair of scissors and adhesive tapes, under his able supervision, musical scores could be extended, shortened, altered, repeated, deleted without leaving behind a trace of any intervention.

Noted film director Kumar Shahani, while working with him during the final phases of his film *Bhavantarana*, shot in Orissa in December 1990, described him as 'an astute editor of sound'; the film revolves around Kelucharan's life and is the only attempt made so far to create a visual document of it. Although the project took nine years to materialize from the time Shahani first approached the Publicity Division of the External Affairs Ministry, and even though it was shot just eight months after Kelucharan's bypass operation, the film nevertheless has successfully captured Kelucharan's art of *abhinaya* in its full maturity.

RETURN TO THE STAGE

THE EARLY EIGHTIES not only saw Kelucharan holding Odissi classes in the form of intensive workshops in Bombay, Delhi and Calcutta at the National Centre for Performing Arts, Gandharva Mahavidyalay and Padatik respectively, but also reappearing quite regularly on the stage along with his disciples at the end of each training session. One of the earliest among such

Kelucharan teaching at the Gandharva Mahavidyalay, New Delhi, in 1979. Madhavi Mudgal is second from left.

TIONAL SEMINAR ON INDIAN DANCE TRADITIONS
RN THEATRE & NATIO
FESTIVAL OF DANCES
Sponsored by
INDUSTRIES Ltd.

performances was the one staged in August 1979 at the small open-air auditorium inside the compound of the Gandharva Mahavidyalay at the conclusion of his first month-long workshop. While he performed '*priye charu sile*' (Radha's cherished love) from the *Gita Govinda*, his senior students Madhavi and Kumkum Lal together rendered the *pallavi* in Raga Khamaj, which had recently been composed in Cuttack with Sanjukta. Kumkum Lal also presented the Oryia *bhajana* '*Badhila jani kshyama*' (Excuse me, I am very oppressed), a poignant *abhinaya* piece composed for Priyambada Mohanty in 1976.

Since this was the first performance to be held on that open-air stage, Kelucharan was asked to perform an elaborate set of rituals before the beginning of the show. It so happened that a little later in the evening, while Kelucharan was rendering his *abhinaya* the lights went off suddenly and the whole place was plunged into darkness for about 10 minutes. All this while Kelucharan remained frozen in the same pose. When finally the lights came back he requested the audience to forgive him since he felt that the black out must have been due to mistakes committed by him while performing the preliminary rituals!

Another stage that was not only inaugurated but also constructed for his show was the open-air theatre at the Padatik Dance Centre in Calcutta. Kelucharan held his first Odissi workshop here in September 1980 and continued to collaborate with them until 1984. In February 1981 he choreographed the *Gita Govinda* dance-drama with the students of the workshop and this was the very first number presented on the newly erected stage in the Centre's courtyard. The production was almost entirely managed by him so as to keep the costs within the limited budget of Rs. 500. He personally supervised the construction of the stage, created the set, placed the lights, stitched most of the dresses and directed the young dancers Aloka, Sutapa, Dipika, Suvra, Dipti, Dipanwita and Paushali in their maiden performace.

From the very first day of the workshop, the Calcutta dancers got a taste of Kelucharan's very tight work schedule: the classes would start around nine in the morning and continued beyond eight in the evening with about an hour's break for lunch brought in containers from home.

'We were not used to this kind of training', recalls one of the workshop participants Sutapa, who had already learnt

Demonstrating the basic steps in Odissi during the International Seminar on Indian Dance Traditions in Calcutta, 1983 (facing page).

Kelucharan in the role of Kaibata, the boatman from the Ramayana.

the preliminaries of the Odissi dance from Muralidhar Majhi before joining Kelucharan. She adds that 'his way of teaching was exacting and scientific; he would be able to stretch our energies to the extreme and get the maximum out of each of us. Then slowly we became so addicted to his style of working that we stopped looking at the watch whenever he was around.'

Devi, a Bengali who had come all the way from Bombay to learn from him, on Protima Bedi's suggestion, comments:

> I was totally new to the Odissi style and I told him so when I first joined the Calcutta workshop. Nevertheless he made me join the beginners class in the morning, the advanced class in the afternoon and taught me the *Gita Govinda ashtapadi* in the evening. Even when my knees started swelling I would not dare to miss his training even for a single moment.

In August 1981 Kelucharan along with his students made his first appearance on a public stage in Calcutta during the Sangeet Research Academy Sangeet Sammelan held at the Kala Mandir. Besides dancing with them in the *mangala charan*, he presented the '*Kuru Yadunandana*' *ashtapadi* and the newly composed sequence *Kaibata prasanga* from Tulsidas' *Sri Ramcharitmanas* in which he portrays the character of the poor boatman Kaibata and his encounter with Rama, Sita and Lakshmana on the bank of the river Ganga. Reviewing the performance Sunil Kothari wrote:

> Performing the *nayika's* various states of mind . . . he showed his artistry in a manner that one rarely sees on the contemporary stage. . . . He is past 50 and balding, he has no external physical endowments nor does he resort to any aid. With simple costume he lit up the areas of poetry creating a parallel poetry in movement and expression on the face. . . . In his concluding portrayal of *Kaibata prasanga* he transmitted Kaibata's emotions so powerfully that many were moved to tears.[1]

During the same year Kelucharan worked closely with Shyamanand Jalan, the theatre director and founder of Padatik, in the production of the Hindi version of *Shakuntala* by Kalidasa. This was to be presented during the Kalidasa Samaroha at Ujjain in Madhya Pradesh. With a cast of about 40 members, the play was meant 'not only to illustrate the word but also to use the body to express the mood', as Shyamanand explains in the booklet brought out for the occasion. Kelucharan directed the movements of all the main characters; he even created two of them, Vidushaka and Kanchuki, the hermaphrodite, and composed the rhythmic structure of the entire play. The music was provided by Girija Devi, the well-known classical singer of the Benaras *gharana*, who also lent her voice to Shakuntala at the moment of her departure from her dear ones.

About Kelucharan's contribution to the work, Shyamanand writes:

> . . . Guruji was a revelation. I knew that he had participated in *jatras* in his boyhood. But his grasp of the fundamental mood, the inner rhythm of the character and the outer rhythm of the movement was amazing. At times I used to start thinking that he was an old timer in the theatre and was resorting to the cliché. But suddenly he would weave a pattern, give it a rhythm and it would become relevant and acceptable to the modern theatre sensibilities. What also impressed us most was his open mind. We used to argue passionately, I used to make my points clearly and at times tactlessly. But he never took offence. He would argue and insist when he would not agree; would immediately change

[1] *The Statesman*, Calcutta, August 1981.

the movements if he agreed; or he would just become a silent spectator. But he had unbounded creativity first and last. He instinctively knew the elements of theatre and theatre acting. He not only gave *mudras* and *charis*, but also conceived some of the characters and both their external and internal movements.

The first workshop at the National Centre for Performing Arts (NCPA) in Bombay was held in December 1981; Kumkum Lal was responsible for this first contact between Kelucharan and the NCPA which turned out to be one of the most lasting and fruitful among all his collaborations. The first performance presented by the guru and his disciples was at the end of the second workshop in June 1982 at the Tata Theatre in the NCPA premises. The students performed the usual sequence of the repertoire, *mangala charan*, *batu* and *pallavi* appositively choreographed in various group patterns which involved a high degree of precision in movement and covering space. In the second part of the programme Kelucharan presented two sets of *ashtapadi* and the *Kaibata prasanga* which today has become a regular feature in almost all his performances. On the rendering of the *ashtapadi* Prakruti Kashyap remarked: 'Kelu Babu executed all these with such profound intensity that when he combed his hair or prepared *chandana* paste or waited in expectancy it was Radha or the friend and not a man with a bald head and pock-marked face'.[2]

But as usual it was the Kaibata's character which stole the show: 'To describe this particular performance is but to enter into empty verbosity. It will suffice to say that the

[2] *Evening News*, Bombay, 12 June 1982.

Portraying vira *(valour)*.

dancer was exalted, his portrayal elevated the aesthete and the common spectator alike, the sense of time and space diminished in eternity of enjoyment and only bliss, bliss of pure devotion pervaded throughout.'[3] This dance sequence, originally composed in 1979 for Oopali Aparajita, could be considered the most original among Kelucharan's interpretations, perhaps with autobiographical connotations in it; the main features of the Kaibata's character, innocence, humility and devotion, are so much an essential part of Kelucharan's nature that one cannot stop seeing the two of them as mutually interchangeable.

Another memorable performance of this period was the one given at the Srisikshia Yatan Hall in Calcutta on the occasion of the Sangeet Shyamala award conferred jointly upon Kelucharan and Girija Devi. On this occasion Kelucharan rendered Tulsidas' Hindi *bhajan 'Janani mei na jiyu bina Rama'* sung and composed by Girija Devi. One cannnot imagine a more effective combination than this to depict the grief stricken Bharata and his pain of separation from his beloved brother Rama exiled by his own mother to pave the way for his coronation. Once again it was a charged combination of humility and devotion which elevated the simple gesture of placing Rama's sandals on the throne to a high degree of dramatic intensity.

A different mood of joyful exuberance would pervade the atmosphere when Girija Devi and Kelucharan shared the stage during the *gulab bari* programmes held during

[3]Ibid.

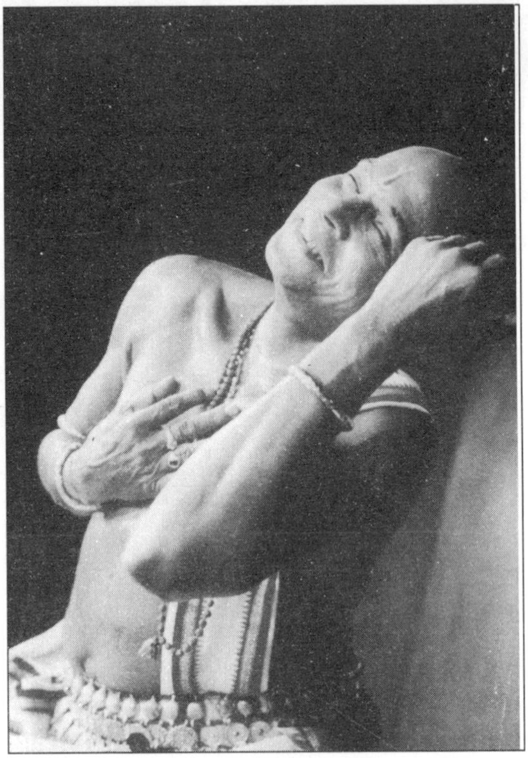

the Holi festivities in Vimla Poddar's house in Calcutta where Birju Maharaj, the renowned Kathak exponent, also joined the celebrations by dancing with Kelucharan to the special songs of Holi. The collaboration between Kelucharan and Girija Devi dates back to the years of the Jayantika meetings in Lokanath Mishra's house. She was in town once to attend a programme at the All India Radio and decided to stay with Lokanath as the latter's wife Binapani was her student. This relationship, which continued all through the years, based on reciprocal feelings of respect and mutual admiration, strengthened even further when Girija Devi's own daughter, Sudha, became Kelucharan's disciple. Whenever possible she even sent him a *rakhi*[4] on the Rakhi Purnima day as sisters do to their elder brothers.

Kelucharan portraying different moods of Kaibata (facing page)

In December 1982 Kelucharan composed and presented (together with the students of the NCPA workshop) the dance-drama *Jatayu Mokshia* (Jatayu's death) with music by Raghunath Panigrahi. Although the tune and development of the story were similar to that of the *Sita Harana* (Sita's abduction) performed by Sanjukta, this new version, in addition, included the episode of the fight between Ravana and the bird Jatayu ending with the highly dramatic climax of the bird's death. The same piece, performed with music by Pundit Jasraj, became a regular feature in Protima Bedi's solo repertoire and was particularly remembered for the Swan Lake style of movement with which Jatayu ends his life: a slow creeper-like motion of the arm which falls on his reclining body after having been mutilated by Ravana's sword.

Kelucharan did not hesitate to utilize in this piece, both in the dance-drama and solo format, elements of the Chhau style in depicting the characters of Ravana and Jatayu, thus enlarging the scope for creativity in the Odissi idiom. His famous rolling on the floor, in the concluding portion of *Kaibata prasanga* when the boatman, out of pure ecstasy and devotion, pays his respects to the very soil upon which Lord Rama has just trod, can also be considered a bold departure from a rigid interpretation of the style. When years later in 1998, he composed for me a solo piece on Ekalavya, the tribal prince of the *Mahabharata* epic, who was denied access to Drona's martial art school because of his lowly caste, Kelucharan drew inspiration for the description of the various ways of handling the weapons

[4] Ceremonial thread which sisters tie around their elder brothers' wrist during the festival of Rakhi Purnima (July-August). It is supposed to be a good-omened gesture.

from the training of the *paika* in the *akhadas* of the Khurda district as recorded by me.

'Don't all these different arts belong to the same cultural milieu? Can you really trace any clear-cut delineation between different artistic expressions?' he would ask while observing with fascination the sinuous and graceful way an eighty-year old *paika* would whirl his sword around his body.

One of the greatest lessons we students ever received from our guru is this rare combination of freedom of creativity and respect for tradition, bound together by an acute aesthetic sense, which allows one to create masterpieces out of every subject he deals with. Once I asked him, 'How would I know while composing if I was well within the tenets of the style or was overstepping it?' The reply that I got is the most important lesson that I received from my guru. Kelucharan said:

> The limits are not dictated by the style but by your aesthetic sense; there is an inner harmony which is common to the movement composed, the underlying music and the context of the meaning to be expressed. If this harmony is not achieved you will instinctively know that something is wrong and you will continue the search for it until that harmony is achieved and when it is realized you will instinctively know.

In Kelucharan's method of teaching the emphasis is definitely on the practical approach and no theory was ever mechanically passed on but extracted from a practical example; his creative process was always laid open before the students, and it was up to them to draw relevant lessons from it. When faced with purely theoretical questions Kelucharan may not come up with brilliant answers whereas his practical demonstrations are always lucid and clear for everybody to see. His way of teaching dance composition to students is to compose all the time in front of their eyes, and as a result almost all his students who learnt from him during these years have not only become performers and teachers but are also involved in the creative aspect as well.

The second dance-drama composed by Kelucharan with the NCPA students was based on the Oriya literary work *Kishora Chandrananda Champu* by Kavisurya Baladeva Ratha. It was presented at the Tata Theatre in May 1983. Though Kelucharan wanted to cast all his senior students in the major roles, finally he was only able to get Kumkum

Kelucharan conducting classes in Japan, 1988 (facing page).

Das who came all the way from Bhubaneswar to perform the role of Krishna. The extremely young and talented Komal Mahuakar became the charming and bashful Radha and Kumkum Lal the witty go-between *sakhi*. An added element was the comic character of Madhu Mangala, Krishna's friend, portrayed histrionically and with a sense of humour by Ratikanta, Kelucharan's son. All the other students of the workshop were cast as the dancing *sakhis*. This ballet, again presented in December of the same year during the Commonwealth Heads of Goverments Meet in New Delhi, had Ratikanta in the role of Krishna, Itishree as Radha and Ananga Dwibedi in the comic role of Madhu Mangala.

The songs in the *Champu* such as '*Leela nidhi he*', '*Khela lola*', '*Ksyamanu kampadharo*', '*Ki hela re*' and others were composed in the distinctive *gotipua* style and Kelucharan often consulted his wife Laxmipriya during the course of the composition. We had glimpses of Guruma's dancing skills during this period, although she would get up to demonstrate a movement or two only after being cajoled by Kelucharan. Even then one could see how graceful and charming she must have been in her youth. Laxmipriya has always been quite reticent about demonstrating her knowledge of dance or even talking of her past life as a dancer.

'I am happy with the popularity that Odissi has achieved nowadays', she once told me, and went on to say that, 'I can never forget how I used to cry and how many times I must have been on the verge of leaving the stage in my youth. People would not talk to me or they would cross to the other side of the road for fear of being polluted by coming near me. So low was the reputation of a dancer in those days!'

In October 1983 she was persuaded by Chetna Jalan to present '*Nahi ki karidela*' at Padatik's small auditorium for a group of invitees. On this occasion Kelucharan danced by her side and it was indeed a rare and an unique experience for the few who were fortunate enough to see her dance.

Bhubaneswar Mishra, who was with the All India Radio in Bombay, took part in the music composition of the *Champu* and a totally new *pallavi* in Raga Belahari was composed for the occasion. This *pallavi* also known as *taranga pallavi*, introduces a peculiar way of sliding the upper portion of the body to resemble a wave-like motion. The composition of all the 34 songs in *Champu* was carried on

'Age no bar': Kelucharan and Laxmipriya dancing at the Padatik Centre, Calcutta, 1983.

years later by Kelucharan during his term of collaboration with the Odissi Research Centre at Bhubaneswar.

At this 1983 workshop in Bombay Bharatanatyam dancer Malavika Sarukkhai was also present; in fact she had already attended a couple of previous workshops conducted in Bombay and it was her intention to continue her Odissi training (which had started in Madras under Ramani Ranjan Jena), with Kelucharan.

It is difficult to say what exactly happened and why Kelucharan, who until then had no objection to teaching her, suddenly changed his mind at the end of this workshop and categorically refused to teach her anymore. Malavika was supposed to take part in the *Champu* ballet as one of the *sakhis*, when all of a sudden she left for Madras after she got a call from her mother. It is possible that Kelucharan was upset at her sudden departure interpreting it as a refusal on her part to be cast in a minor role. Or perhaps, as he put it, he did not want to come between her and Ramani, her previous teacher, or, and this could perhaps be the main reason, Laxmipriya, Kelucharan's wife, was not pleased with her for some reason and Kelucharan was compelled not to teach her more for the sake of maintaining peace in the family.

This was the second 'glamorous' break-up after the first one with Sonal in the early seventies. While Sonal, although extremely hurt by it, took it as a challenge and reacted by learning from other gurus and finally by being on her own, Malavika, after all her attempts to be accepted back had failed, finally left the Odissi style and concentrated solely on Bharatanatyam.

All of us, in the course of our training, have experienced Kelucharan's temper and sudden threats but we have learnt to accept them as temporary rebukes and not as final statements. Forgiveness was always granted if one said 'sorry' with sincerity and in good faith.

Only on very few occasions have the outbursts turned out to be definitive, as in the case of Protima Bedi in 1993 and Kumkum Das in 1995. While differences with the first was again related to problems involving Kelucharan's family, this time not his wife but his son Ratikanta was at the centre of it, the second was caused for the same reasons which prompted Kelucharan to leave his guru Mohansundar Dev Goswami and then later the Kala Vikash Kendra: the feeling of being overruled or taken for granted. Kelucharan however never severed his ties before having given all his attention, energy and all that he knew of his art and having put the person or the institution in a position to be able to continue and flourish independently. He says: 'My relations with the students is like that of a father with his kids: he helps them until they are in need, and when he understands that they have reached a stage when they can be independent, he steps aside.'

Kelucharan's sensibility as a teacher is a perpetual source of wonder for his students; he has an inborn sense of discrimination which ensures that nothing escapes his attention. A slight inflexion in the voice, expression of the face or an unusual detail in the attire is immediately perceived and retained in his memory. His acquaintance with each of the students is primarily based on their 'physicality';

Kelucharan in a comic interlude during classes (facing page).

he 'reads' their personality through their gaits, gestures, talks or reactions. He would come forward to make the shy student comfortable and crush without pity the inflated ego of the proud one. If a person was sad, Kelucharan would cheer him up by cracking jokes, and he would not tolerate jealousy among his students for any reason.

His ways of correcting the mistakes of students include hitting with a stick, throwing the stick from a distance, addressing the students with epithets such as 'pig', 'horse', 'elephant', '*sala*', or a symbolic order to leave the class (which, if really executed will make him even more angry). Tears are not tolerated, especially after a rebuke, as also signs of fatigue, casual attitude or excessive eagerness.

He is an indefatigable storyteller; in between teaching and demonstrations he would narrate countless anecdotes from his past, tales from mythology or his personal philosophy of life. During these long intervals in which the narrative vein prevails, the students from their standing position would start sliding down one by one into a squatting one until brought back to their feet by a sudden stroke of the stick.

In the class everybody is treated as a child, no matter how old he or she may be. Sonal narrates how, after about twenty years, when finally she returned to Orissa to take part in the dance-drama *Konarka* to be staged by the Odissi Research Centre during the Konarka Festival, it was exactly how it used to be two decades earlier: when she used to doze off, exhausted by the late hour and the interminable rehearsals, in the underground greenroom of the amphitheatre, she was suddenly woken up by an energetic slap and confronted by Kelucharan asking her: '*Kana jhia, ethi saibhaku assiciu*?' (What for, did you come here to sleep?). The mighty and temperamental Sanjukta also became docile and submissive in his presence.

His reactions at times may seem out of proportion but in most cases they turn out to be meaningful when looked at in retrospect. I have once been the target of an excessive outburst of his anger; the reason which caused it apparently was not all that serious but nevertheless Kelucharan would not relent: I was forbidden to continue with the workshop, no matter how much I tried to ask for forgiveness.

'I don't know why, but I feel that I cannot teach you any more', he kept telling me. It was the summer of 1985, I had been in Orissa for six continuous years away from Italy.

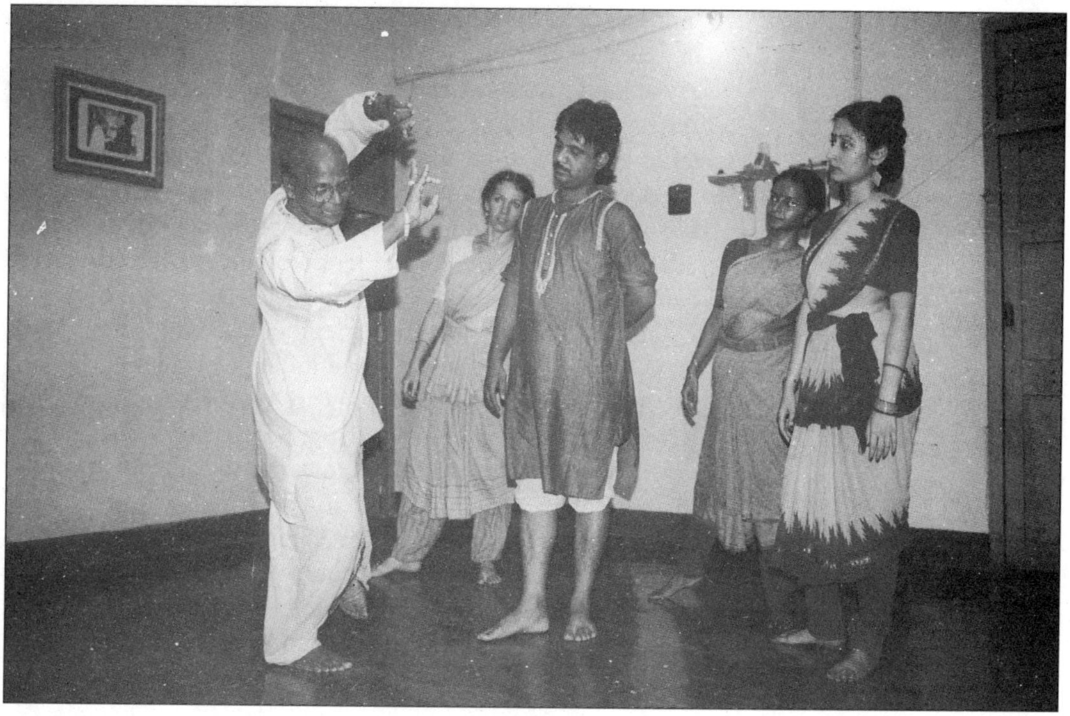

Training session in Bhubaneswar, 1989.

There had been an invitation that year to perform somewhere in Europe, but I had decided at the last moment not to travel since I did not want to miss the summer workshop. Facing the prospect of having to remain outside the classroom unable to enter, I wondered if I should take up that offer. It turned out to be a good thing. I renewed contact with my country, my people, and I was happy that I could share with them the art form and knowledge that I had acquired in these six years. But the amazing thing was that when I came back after about a month and went to Kelucharan, he received me as if nothing had ever happened and eagerly enquired about my performance.

If the classes were punctuated by rebukes, comic interludes were also not lacking. He is an extra-ordinary mimic, his imitation of the gait, gesture and mannerisms of his students is among the best in his repertoire. The most amusing take off is of a man in a crowded bus with an urgent need to clear his bowels.

His sense of humour would emerge in most unexpected ways and circumstances and he would not even spare himself. When in 1988 he came to know that he had been chosen for the Padma Bhushan award he was conducting classes in Delhi. The students present there congratulated him and celebrated in a big way; the same thing happened in Calcutta and at the Odissi Research Centre in Bhubaneswar. In Cuttack, since there were no students attending classes in his home during that period, I ordered a floral tableau with Padma Bhushan written on it and fixed it on his door post. I could not be present when he arrived, but as soon as he heard me approaching the next day, he took out the tableau, held it in front of his face, and started dancing!

All his students fondly remember the long hours spent in the classroom during the summer workshops. During this period one would be unaware of the passage of time having left all problems and preoccupations outside the door. No matter how many times Kelucharan had already demonstrated a detail or had gone through the nuances of an expression, he would still be able to hold our attention totally. The same gesture is repeated by him over and over again, the same movement examined in its constituent units, analysed in its minutes detail, and is presented each time with fresh nuances. The oppressive heat of the summer

Laxmipriya giving finishing touches to Kelucharan's make-up.

With Ravi Shankar at his residence in San Diego in USA, 1996.

season would be followed by the steaming humidity of the pre-monsoon days which in turn would finally give way to the unabated fury of the rainy season. Still nothing inside the room would change; undaunted by the elements Kelucharan would continue to conduct the classes.

The evening *arati* at the small mandir in one corner of the house and the meals served to us sitting in a semicircle on the classroom floor by Laxmipriya, were all part of the daily routine. Students from Bombay, Delhi and Calcutta left behind their sophisticated lifestyle and very soon got used to the indigenous Oriya food and way of living.

Laxmipriya handles all the domestic chores with ease. While Kelucharan is in-charge of the training sessions of the workshop participants, she ably handles all their problems of food and lodging. There is no limit to the number of students at the workshops and does not involve formalities such as registration or enrolment; everybody is welcome to join and each participant finds a suitable place in the class depending on his or her standard.

Senior students happily attend these classes over and over again along with the newcomers, the talented among them are allowed to join the advanced classes. During the late

hours one would assist in the creation of new compositions essentially for Sanjukta or other senior students. It is indeed a rewarding experience to watch Kelucharan at his creative best.

With German choreographer Pina Baush in Avignon, 1995 (facing page).

Kelucharan is usually in a jovial and relaxed mood during his foreign trips. Always attentive, curious, interested in whatever is happening around him, trying to understand, infer, correlate and absorb new experiences.

'A dancer has to possess the rhythm, the body and the spirit. The guru has to possess this and all the rest. For this he cannot stop learning and researching', Kelucharan remarked to a journalist in France days after receiving the title of 'Officer of the Order of Art and Culture' from the French Ministry of Culture in 1995.[5]

While most members of the troupe would be vey fussy about the food and not venture into any unknown territory, Kelucharan on the contrary, barring beef, would enjoy eating all sorts of foodstuff.

Students remember how during his trip to Russia for the Festival of India in August 1987, he promptly responded to an invitation to dance by a big Russian woman, and holding his dhoti folded up like a skirt, started rotating all around the floor imitating the Russian folk style, encouraging all of them to join in.

'One day, while I was standing near him, I was attracted by a very handsome Russian young man', remembers Jhelum, a student from Bombay, 'and I started staring at him. Guruji looked at both of us for some time and then asked me why I was looking at him. I said that I found him handsome', and he promptly said: 'Why, am I not handsome too?'

In the summer of 1988, in one small village of south Italy, where our performance was supposed to take place, we discovered to our dismay that the wooden stage had been badly damaged at several places because of the jumping around by the Brasilian dancers the previous day. The organizers were in a fix because, being a holiday, no worker could be found. Although their entire discussion was conducted in Italian, Kelucharan could make out what the problem was, and without wasting a breath he rushed down and was already on his back beneath the stage with a hammer and nails trying to fix the broken planks.

In the eighties, during his foreign tours, Kelucharan besides accompanying his students on the pakhawaj, started

[5] *Le Meridional*, 7 July 1995.

Kelucharan wearing wig in his reappearance on stage in the early 1980s, in Benaras, along with Kumkum Das (facing page).

performing himself, leaving the dance critics astonished that in an art that takes its toll even at the early age of 30, how could a man of 60 move with such grace and sensitivity.

'Mohapatra's program was a revelation', wrote Dick Moore in *Marinscope* in December 1985. 'Watching him one might be reminded of Nijinsky (for the same magnificent sinuous torso and arms) and Chaplin (Mohapatra is one of the most inspired gestural actors I've ever seen).'[6]

Eleven years later, in September 1996, during another American tour, this time on the occasion of his seventieth birthday celebration, he was once again compared to the legendary Nijinsky by Jennifer Dunning of the *New York Times*: 'Dramatic gesture was pure dance here, with his fluting hands seeming to contain some nectar and his presence recalling Nijinsky's sensuous abandon.'[7]

In the first two Festivals of India, which Kelucharan attended, the first one in London in 1982 and the second in Paris in 1986, in a duet with two of his senior students, Sanjukta and Kumkum, he performed the *ashtapadi 'yahi Madhava yahi Kesava'* followed by *'priye charu sile'*. These choreographic variants of the solo compositions of the same *ashtapadi*, were first introduced by Kelucharan during a performance in Varanasi in October 1981, where he danced in tandem with Kumkum Das.

In this maiden appearance, Kelucharan, perhaps still a little insecure about the public's reaction to his bald head, wore a black wig which made him look much younger. Quite soon though the wig was discarded at the insistence of his senior students and never was it needed again!

In the same performance Kelucharan also danced the *'Kuru Yadhunandana'* song with two of his students, Aloka and Pranati, portraying in the background the same dancing poses which he was enacting in front. The same presentation was repeated several times in the subsequent years especially on bigger stages. The frozen poses portrayed on an elevated platform in the background, by adding a pictorial dimension to the plastic one, represented a synthesis of Kelucharan's own experience in both.

With the number of students as well as opportunities to perform increasing steadily, the dance pieces, which had originally been created as solo compositions, during these years were re-choreographed by Kelucharan for group formations. Among the ones most often presented in group formations were the *batu* and *Dashavatara*, which

[6] *Marinscope*, 21-8 December 1985.
[7] *The New York Times*, 30 September 1996.

Performing with students during a Seminar on Jayadev in Bhubaneswar, 1984.

underwent countless number of variations, although maintaining the same musical score and basic features. The *pallavi*, or items of pure *nritta*, when presented by more than one dancer, were often just identical presentation of the same movements distributed in space, whereas the dance pieces which required *abhinaya* came closer to a dramatic format, with different characters being assigned to each of the dancers.

Kelucharan's association with the Odissi Research Centre dates back to its inception in 1984. The project was the brainchild of his senior student Kumkum Das, an official of the Indian Postal Service, who that year was very briefly posted on deputation as the Director of Culture. Kumkum had stopped giving performances during the first few years after her marriage, but had always kept in touch with Kelucharan.

The last composition which Kelucharan did for her in 1972, just before her marriage, had been the Oriya song *'Ahe nila saila'*. It was a prayer to Lord Jagannath penned by the Muslim poet Salabhega wherein he depicts the popular episodes of Vishnu rescuing an elephant from the crocodile's jaws, Draupadi from the lust of the Kaurava brothers, and

Prahalada from his greedy father Hiranyakashipu. On Kumkum's return to the dance stage in 1978, Kelucharan was requested by her father to compose a song from the *Bichitra Ramayana* written by the Oriya poet Biswanath Khuntia in the eighteenth century. Kelucharan chose the episode of the golden deer (*hema harini*) and of Sita lamenting Rama's loss while being carried away by Ravana (*eh bana giri, he lata giri*) and combined both the songs in a single dance piece of about 25 minutes.

Again, in 1979, Kelucharan composed for Kumkum a *pallavi* in the Raga Hamsadhwani and choreographed the famous dialogue between Krishna and Arjuna from the *Bhagavad Gita* for a performance in Bombay in the same year. Both the compositions had brilliant musical scores by Bhubaneswar Mishra. The *Bhagavad Gita* piece was later, rendered as a duet by Kumkum (as Krishna) and Sanjukta (as Arjuna) for the Mukteswar Festival in Bhubaneswar in 1984.

Somehow the long years spent away from the dance scene had left a question mark on Kumkum's career as a performer for it would have been difficult for her at this point to compete with the increasing number of young dancers emerging on the Odissi dance scene. On the other hand, her experience as an administrator and her closeness to the government machinery could be useful for providing the infrastructure and the funds for her plans of establishing a centre devoted to the codification and documentation of the Odissi dance. This work had not been accomplished by the Jayantika meetings and nothing more had been tried in this direction since.

Right from the beginning Kelucharan had been extremely enthusiastic about the idea and agreed to work for the centre, at an initial honorarium of Rs. 4,000 per month, along with the other two important personalities involved in the revival of the Odissi dance, music composer Bhubaneswar Mishra and Odissi singer Balakrishna Das.

Kelucharan as usual gave his best during his ten years of collaboration at the centre, while continuing his other activities outside the centre. Under his able guidance, within a couple of years, a good group of young dancers who had joined the research centre for further training had become a regular performing unit and the centre started to present regular shows both within and outside the state. Apart from reworking the existing pieces in the repertoire for group

presentation, Kelucharan proposed to include *Krishna Gatha* the way it used to be performed by the Kala Vikash Kendra troupe and the newly choreographed *Ekalavya*, conceived in a dance-drama format. In the latter, he performed as Drona while Kumkum did the role of the tribal prince Jhara. During his years at the centre, senior male dancers, who had learnt the art from Kelucharan at the Kala Vikash Kendra in the sixties and had by now started teaching in different places, had the opportunity to come back to him during the masters' courses, specially conceived for polishing their technique, updating their style and teaching them new dance pieces.

The dance-dramas composed by him during this period for the government sponsored annual Konarka Dance Festival included: *Chandrabhaga* (1989), *Chandrika* (1990), *Dasanana* (1991), *Konarka* (1993) and *Yagnyaseni* (1994).

The codification work envisaged by Kumkum aimed at creating a systematic and unified grammar of Odissi dance by collecting all that had been done till then in the practical field and extracting from it the basic elements to be classified and assigned a name. Besides the codification of the style, an attempt was also made towards the development of a full-fledged system of dance notation, to which Kelucharan contributed immensely by meticolously drawing entire sequences of dance movements with all the detailed foot, hand and torso positions.

Although in course of time other gurus such as Pankaj Charan Das and Mahadev Rout were also temporarily roped in, it was Kelucharan's style which was mostly explored and utilized for classification. This created controversies and it was probably one of the reasons why the grammar codified by the centre could not really find a larger circulation.

In 1987, Kelucharan along with his wife decided to leave his Cuttack residence and to shift to a government alloted quarter in Bhubaneswar. The decision was prompted by a difficult situation which arose in the family due to frictions between the daughter-in-law and mother-in-law. Kelucharan, for the sake of maintaining peace and tranquillity, left the house to the young couple and embarked on setting up a new home in a new surrounding.

The exodus was a sad sight; Lord Jagannath and all the other divinities were ceremonially removed from the little temple, packed in a box and placed in the luggage rack of

Kelucharan with his guru Pankaj Charan Das at the Odissi Research Centre in 1986 (facing page).

the car along with suitcases, bags, containers and kitchen utensils. The overloaded Padmini car resembled a gypsy caravan ready to take off for some far away destination. From then on, except for a few days during the summer of that same year when Kelucharan came back during daytime to conduct classes for the local students, neither the stomping feet resounded in the house at Cuttack nor the evening *arati* was performed accompanied by the students' chorus at the door of the little temple. None of the onlookers (except the daughter-in-law), were able to hold back tears at the sight of the two old people leaving their home, but Kelucharan looked extremely composed.

'My home is where Jagannath is', he said, knowing full well that wherever he went, his students would follow him. It took him just a few months to transform an ordinary and bare government quarter into a pulsating and vital centre, with a small garden in front, a little temple in the corner of a room and enough space for the dance classes.

But the tensions in the family and his tendency to overwork did take their toll. In August 1989 Kelucharan was admitted to the intensive care unit of the Capital Hospital in Bhubaneswar for a mild heart attack. Students of the Odissi Research Centre took turns to look after him round the clock while he was recuperating. In April of the following year, when he went to the Birla Heart Centre in Calcutta for a check-up, he was straightaway operated upon a triple bypass by the young and competent heart specialist Dr Devi Shetty. As soon as the news of his surgery spread, students started pouring in and enquiries came from all quarters. Biju Patnaik, the then Orissa chief minister and a great personal admirer of Kelucharan, sent a special emissary to Calcutta to hand over to him a cheque of Rs. 1,40,000 to cover the entire cost of his bypass operation.

For about four months after the operation Kelucharan led a more regulated life; the innumerable cups of tea were stopped, the chewing of *pan* was considerably reduced, and both the meals were taken at the proper time and at night the lights were put out soon after midnight.

I had the privilege to work with him during that summer on the *nava rasa* (nine sentiments) a piece based on the Shiva mythology, which I had asked him to compose. Kelucharan was working on the topic of the *nava rasa* for the first time since he had not found until then a suitable subject to relate to it. The episodes taken from Shiva's story to illustrate each of the nine basic sentiments as they are conceived in the Indian aesthetic theory, seemed to appeal to him; in fact he retained the same subject while dancing to the flute of Pundit Chaurasia for Kumar Shahani's film on his life in December of the same year.

Just one month before his first heart attack, at the end of July 1989, Kelucharan had been felicitated in Bangalore during a function organized by his student Protima Bedi to launch the idea behind her dream project: the construction of a dance village, Nrityagram. Protima had planned that all the seven styles of classical dances would be taught free of cost to a select number of pupils residing under one roof with their respective gurus. The first *gurukul*, the Odissi one, was finally inaugurated in April 1990 and Kelucharan, unable to go himself due to his ill health, first sent a male student and then his own son Ratikanta as a permanent teacher. He himself visited the village periodically for holding practical workshops until the year 1993, when a misunderstanding between Protima and Ratikant put an end to Kelucharan's collaboration.

This was not the first time that, for the sake of his son, Kelucharan discontinued teaching at an institution; something similar had happened at Padatik in Calcutta the moment it became clear that his son would not be accepted as his substitute. He has often been accused of promoting his own son at the expense of other male dancers; the low attendance of male dancers in his classes has been seen by some as proof of his lack of interest in any male dancer other than his son.

Although these accusations are totally baseless, there is no doubt that Kelucharan has all along been very attentive towards his son's upbringing, especially because of Laxmipriya's extreme concern about it. On his part, Ratikanta, sensing quite soon the great responsibility that would fall on his shoulders as the heir of such a great master, took quite a few years before concentrating on perpetuating his father's legacy. Caught between a very possessive mother and the high expectations of his father, he took quite some time to find his own direction.

He started attending dance classes around the late seventies when he was about 13 years old and I remember how in those days he would quit the dance class as often as he possibly could, and how he would always be found in his hideouts and brought back to discipline by his vigilant parents. He had however an inborn talent and could pick up things quite easily, and this was perhaps what gave him a sense of over-confidence. During his childhood, till he was 10 years old, Ratikanta saw very little of his father because of his long trips to Delhi and Bombay for programmes and workshops. He was left under the care of a certain Srinivasan Mohanty, a scientist and playwright, whom Laxmipriya had come to know during the years she was frequenting the All India Radio for acting in plays, and who had come to stay in their house in the early sixties. Srinivasan was quite a learned man and whatever formal knowledge of English and Hindi Ratikanta acquired was largely because of the scientist.

Ratikanta remembers two episodes from his childhood which left an indelible impression on him. He was about eight years old when one day his father had tied him to a *jhui* tree using the creeper as cords, and left him there for about four hours in the sun as punishment for having stolen Rs. 5 from his pocket. Ratikanta had been betrayed by the ice cream man who got suspicious when he saw the boy offering ice cream to all his friends and informed his father.

On the second occasion, few years later, Keulcharan asked Ratikanta to play along with him a certain sequence of *bols* on the pakhawaj but, while he succeeded in playing it in the first two speeds, the *vilambit* and *madhyam* one, he failed in the *dhrut*. Ratikanta had learnt to play the pakhawaj almost entirely on his own by observing his father teach the elder male students. And that was the first test he had to undergo. Kelucharan got furious at his inability to perform in the third speed and instructed him to practice regularly for ten minutes both in the mornings and evenings for a full month and then to come to him again. 'It will not be sufficient for you to be my son to be able to carve a name for yourself; whatever standard you achieve will depend entirely on your practice', Kelucharan told him when, after one month, he passed the test successfully.

Eventually in the course of time, Ratikanta turned out to be not only a proficient accompanist on the pakhawaj but also an outstanding interpreter of highly dramatic characters such as Ravana and Hanuman. His interpretation of the monkey god in dance-dramas based on the *Ramayana*, became more and more articulate with each performance and gave him the opportunity and honour to perform this role every year, from 1985 onward, in the prestigious Sankat Mochana Festival at Benaras.

Besides the preoccupation with his son's career, Kelucharan was equally anxious about his marriage. When all the efforts at finding for his son a suitable bride among the Odissi dancers failed, both he and his wife had to accept Ratikanta's choice: an Oriya Christian girl, a few years older than him, who occasionally acted on stage and in television. It took almost a couple of years for Kelucharan and his wife to get reconciled to this choice, but finally a compromise was reached when Ritha agreed to convert to Hindu religion. At this point a marriage ritual was performed first at the Arya Samaj Mandir and then repeated in the Oriya style at Kelucharan's house. Kelucharan attended to all the preparations for the function in his usual meticulous way, beaming with excitement and joy all through the ritual.

For the second time Kelucharan had broken the rules of 'marrying within the caste' in his family; the first time by marrying Laxmipriya who was not a *chitrakara jhia*, and now by accepting a Christian daughter-in-law in his household. His relatives, expecially his elder brother Ekadasi and his younger one Bansidhar, did not approve of this compromise and decided not to attend the marriage ceremony.

Unfortunately Kelucharan's happiness did not last long; after only a month of living together, tensions started to surface between Ritha and Laxmipriya and for the sake of peace Kelucharan decided to leave the Cuttack house to the young couple.

Years of tension followed, both for Ratikanta, who had to shuttle between Cuttack and Bhubaneswar to be able to stay with his wife on the one hand, and to work with his father on the other, and for Kelucharan and his wife who were denied the joy of living with their son.

The first daughter, Charu, had been given in marriage several years ago to a man from Bhadrak who, after getting a son from her, married a second time and started neglecting her. Once in a while Charu would come home to her parents determined not to return any more to her in-law's house, and her husband would regularly come and take her back. It seemed for some time that, while the outside world was showering honours and praises on Kelucharan and his fame was increasing day by day, his own children were letting him down.

After his father's heart attack, Ratikanta started to show more concern for his role in the family and his duties towards his parents. While his marriage with Ritha was entering into a critical phase, in the early nineties he became close to one of the dancers whom Kelucharan had selected for his German tour. This new relationship found both the parents agreeable and opened up a new phase in Kelucharan's family life. Ratikanta finally got a divorce from his first wife, and settled down with Sujata. Being a dancer herself, the new daughter-in-law began to play an important role in the family.

When Kelucharan decided to leave the Odissi Research Centre in December 1994, the time was ripe for him to finally channelize his energies towards something of his own instead of diverting it, as he had done till now, towards institutions established by others. Kelucharan sent his resignation to the centre soon after the staging of the dance-drama *Yagnyaseni* which he had recently composed to inaugurate the 1994 Konarka Dance Festival.

As usual, Kelucharan had worked round the clock for the composition of the ballet, keeping the entire group of dancers and musicians awake late in the night during the entire period of rehearsals. There was nothing new about this and everybody was more than accustomed to his style of functioning. What struck as a discordant note was the heated arguments Kelucharan had with Kumkum a few hours before going to the stage, regarding the very issue of the interpretation of the text. Kumkum indirectly accused Kelucharan of not being able to interpret the actual intentions of the writer. The script was based on a modern interpretation of the Draupadi myth as depicted in the homonymous novel by the contemporary writer Pratibha Roy. Many discussions had taken place in the presence of the writer at the beginning of the rehearsals, and Kelucharan felt that at this point an accusation of that nature was an insult to his creativity.

He probably felt that he was not needed or trusted any more and he decided there and then to withdraw from the centre. The further accusations launched at him by Kumkum soon after the show attributing the poor success of the performance to his frenetic way of rehearsing and to a disproportionate role given to his son in the production, made him determined to leave the centre.

During the ten years of his association with the centre, Kelucharan had contributed immensely to its growth by training numerous dancers, accompanying them on stage, composing new dance pieces, allowing video recordings while demonstrating the basic stances of the style, and providing sketches and diagrams for developing the dance notation system. Besides, he gave a new lease of life to Kumkum as a dancer by placing her in a position to continue on her own in her new role as a researcher and composer.

The idea of founding Srjan, his own institution, had started to crystallize in 1993 when his students in Bombay organized a dance programme for collecting the initial capital to form the trust. By now Kelucharan had left the government quarters and was busy finishing his new house in the Bhimatangi area in the old part of Bhubaneswar. As the institution grew, the house also kept growing, until from an initial single bedroom house it became one having two classrooms, five bedrooms, and nine bathrooms. While the father looked after the planning and construction of the building (as usual without consulting any architect or engineer!), the son managed the administrative and organizational wing and the daughter-in-law taught the young local students whose number kept increasing day by day.

Although tensions in the family could not be totally eliminated, due to friction creeping up now and then between Laxmipriya and the new daughter-in-law, nevertheless the running of the institution kept everybody busy. Under the dynamic direction of Ratikanta, by now totally devoted to the cause, Srjan has developed into a pulsating dance centre, where old and new students receive training and have participated in the dance-dramas produced since 1994. Among these are: *Utkala mauda mani* (The gem in the crown of Utkala) (1994), *Chand Ashoka* (The cruel Ashoka) (1995), *Kurukshetra* (1996), *Sudama Daridra Bhanjana* (Who destroyed Sudama's poverty), *Mathamani pradana* (The best jewel for the head), *Sita Harana* (Sita's Abduction) and *Balya Leela* (1998).

The Bhimatangi house is now big enough to house twenty students at a time and the new part of the building includes an office where proper cash books, attendance and salary registers are kept. The young students wear uniforms and at the end of the year appear for regular examinations conducted by the local Sangeet Natak Akademi.

While all this is the responsibility of Ratikant, Kelucharan still prefers to operate in the old style; individual compositions for senior students are still carried on in the drawing room, at any time of the day and night, without institutional formalities. He sits in the classroom only during the June-July workshop when students assemble from all over and classes are conducted all day long. For the rest of the year he leaves the floor to the younger people and when not on the move for some programme or the other, he is busy with construction work. After the completion of the house at Bhubaneswar he has now diverted his attention to his dream project: the construction of a small temple, in his native village, around the tree that has been since time immemorial the abode of Ma Bhuasuni, the goddess to whom he had been offered as a five-year-old.

To supervise the work on the temple he goes to Raghurajpur every morning by car, along with the masons who are by now almost a part of his family, and stays there the whole day. The construction plan envisaged by him keeps the old tree intact, and maintain its harmony with the surroundings. Money for the temple is donated by him and the students, and each donation, no matter how small, is religiously noted down in a small account book.

At the age of seventy-five and with all the major honours having been conferred upon him, including the Padma Vibhushan award which he received in March 2000, Kelucharan is still as keen to learn and absorb from life as he used to be when he was a kid. He absorbs, recreates and shares his wonders with whomsoever he meets. Not only dancers but people from all walks of life are irresistibly attracted towards him. He is accessible to everyone; his strength being his humility and devotion. He dances on stage as if possessed by a divine spirit which acts through him; never repeating himself, always recreating with total involvement.

For his disciples he is like god. In Malaysia the artists of the Temple of Fine Arts a few years ago, performed a puja by installing him in place of the deity. The citation read: 'Thee Divine Lord of Dance receive our deepest joy for having our wish fulfilled, our dream comes true. A Great Master has come. By Divine will, Guru Kelucharan Mohapatra has come to bless us with his loving presence. . . .'

Recently his own guru, Pankaj Babu, after a very moving performance by Kelucharan, garlanded his worthy disciple in a spontaneous gesture by removing the garland from the statue of Krishna that had been kept on one side of the stage.

Kelucharan received all these demonstrations of love with grace and offered everything to his beloved Lord Jagannath; on stage, as in life, devotion filled his gestures and radiated from him on all those who had the fortune to come in contact with him.

GLOSSARY

Abhinaya Darpana: treatise on gestures and postures used in dance written by Nandikeswara in the third century.
abhinaya: expression of emotional states through gestures in dance.
akhada: space where physical training is imparted.
anasara: fortnight during which the idols of Jagannath, Balabhadra, Subhadra are concealed from public view (May-June).
arati: offering of light to the deity.
ashram: hermitage.
ashtapadi: poem consisting of eight stanzas.
asura: demon.
Bada Danda: wide road which runs from the Jagannath Temple to the Gundicha Temple at Puri. Pilgrims pull the chariot of Lord Jagannath along this road at the time of the Car Festival.
Bhagavad Gita: sacred Hindu text composed about 200 BC and incorporated into the *Mahabharata*.
bhajan: devotional singing.
bidi: cheap leaf cigarettes.
chaddar: type of shawl.
Chaitanya Mahaprabhu: founder of Vaishnavism, a *bhakti* cult centred on devotion to a personal God.
chandana: sandal paste.
changu: a percussion instrument.
chari: movements of the feet.
chatasali: village school.
Chhau dance: semi-classical dance having its origins in the practice of martial art of Orissa.

chitrakara: traditional painters of Orissa.
darshana: sight, vision.
Dashavatara: ten incarnations of Lord Vishnu.
devadasi: temple dancers married to the deity through a special ritual.
dharamshala: rest house for pilgrims.
dholak: percussion instrument.
dhrupad: vocal composition of the Hindustani system of music.
Dwaraka: ancient kingdom ruled by Lord Krishna.
gamcha: cotton towel.
Gita Govinda: twelfth century Sanskrit poetical work by poet Jayadeva describing the love of Radha and Krishna.
gharana: affiliated group with a distinctive traditional style of dance and music.
gotipua: boy dancers dressed as girls.
gua: areca nuts.
gurukul: ancient Indian system of education.
Hindustani: system of music belonging to north India.
Jagannath: incarnation of Lord Vishnu and chief deity of Orissa.
jatra: folk play.
jugalbandi: two artists performing together.
kadamba: flowering tree made famous by its association with Lord Krishna's amorous dalliance with milkmaids from Vrindavan.
Kali: an incarnation of Goddess Durga.
Karnatic: system of music belonging to south India.
Kartika: holy lunar month in the Hindu calendar.
kirtan: same as Sankirtana.
Konarka: famous twelfth century Sun Temple of Orissa.
Kumara Purnima: full moon day in the lunar month of *Aswin* in the Hindu calendar (September-October).
kumbha: pot, vessel.
lasya: graceful dance attributed to Goddess Parvati, Lord Shiva's consort.
leela: play dealing with incidents in the life of Lord Krishna.
Lokanath: appellative of Lord Shiva.
mahari: the Oriya name given to the *devadasi* or servant of God.
mancha pravesh: first stage performance.
mangala charan: propitious beginning; first item of the Odissi dance repertoire.
matra: single count.

mokshya: literallly means 'liberation'; it is the last item of the Odissi dance repertoire.
mukuta: crown.
murti: idol.
naga: type of mendicant.
nartaki: female dancer.
Natya Shastra: treatise on dramatic arts attributed to Bharata Muni.
nayika: heroine, embodying the romantic concept of the beloved.
pallavi: item of *nritta* or 'pure dance' which is usually performed on stage after the *mangala charan*.
pallu: end border of a sari.
pata chitra: traditional painting of Orissa.
patta: handmade canvas.
pothi: palm-leaf manuscripts.
puja bhog: food offered to a deity.
raga: modal system of Indian classical music.
raj durbar: court of a king.
rasi: constellation.
Ras Leela: play dealing with the amorous sports of Krishna with the milkmaids of Vrindavan.
Ratha Yatra: Car Festival held in Puri.
sakhi: female companion.
sanchari (bhava): transitory states meant to highlight the permanent ones in a dramatic representation.
sangeeta: term encompassing three arts: singing, playing of instruments and dancing.
Sankirtana: devotional singing in chorus accompanied by playing of percussion instruments.
satwika (bhava): temperamental states caused by the concentration of the mind on an emotion.
seva: service.
sevayat: servitors in the temples of Hindu Gods and Goddesses.
shastric: relating to scriptures.
singhasana: throne or seat of a deity.
sitar: plucked lute-type stringed instrument.
sloka: Sanskrit hymn.
tala: metric system of Indian classical music.
tala-patra: palm-leaf.
tandava: powerful and virile dance attributed to Lord Shiva.
Upendra Bhanja: eighteenth century Oriya poet famous for his stylistic virtuosity.

Urvashi: one of the celestial dancers.
ustad: maestro; master musician; teacher of music.
Vasanta Utsava: spring festival.
vidwan: accomplished musician, scholar.
Yagnyaseni: another name for Draupadi, wife of the five Pandava brothers in the *Mahabharata*.
zamindar: landlord.
zari: intricate lace-work.

APPENDICES

APPENDIX 1

THE LAST JOURNEY

Guruji passed away on 7 April 2004 at 10.30 in the morning. It all happened within a short span of time. While coming out of the bathroom that morning he felt unwell and started perspiring; his son Ratikanta immediately took him in the car towards the main hospital in Bhubaneswar which is just a 15 minutes drive from his house. On the way, while reclining his head on his daughter-in-law's lap, he breathed his last. I came to know of his death immediately and reached his house at about the same time as their car was returning from the hospital. The images of what followed are still fresh in my mind. While we were dressing up his body in a fresh *dhoti*, putting vermilion on his forehead and decorating him with flowers, I remembered the many times and he had dressed up students and helped put on ornaments during his lifetime. His hands now inert along his sides still had that peculiar elegant alertness which fascinated me from the very beginning. How many types of work I had seen them doing; mending, repairing, tying, mixing cement and sand, plastering walls, cleaning the house drainage, decorating, playing, drawing, dancing and all through it they never ceased to transmit a particular kind of assurance. They seemed to be able to solve any kind of problem. I could not take my eyes away from them; I kept holding one of them in my hands as if he was just sleeping, waiting to wake up any moment. Quite soon the news of Kelu Babu's death spread around and people started pouring in. A profusion of flowers kept on being offered to his body; his pink short *kurta* totally submerged by them. The wooden cot on which he was placed had to be removed for making space for two huge ice blocks. Later sand had to be spread around on the floor to absorb the melting ice. The mourners kept increasing, and I had to let go of his hand. I looked around, and there were some known faces of old students among the many in the crowd whom I did not know. Everybody knew Guruji; his fame is so wide spread that any common man, of the streets in Orissa knew who Kelucharan Mohapatra was. He had always time and patience for anybody; in fact he could interest even a rickshaw puller or a mason to the peculiarities of the Odissi dance form! Among the people around his cot I saw one rickshaw puller searching for something to offer; not having brought any flowers, he finally took out from the folds of his *dhoti* a packet of *bidis* and a match box and then with folded hands offered them to him!

Seventy-eight is usually not considered a premature age for dying, but in his case none of us remembered his actual age. Fourteen years ago he had recovered from a triple by-pass in the course of just six months; only the scar visible on his bare chest while dancing on stage was a sad reminder of the operation he had undergone. Few days hence he would have left for Varanasi to perform during the Sankat Mochan festival; a week later he was to leave for Paris for a month long tour and on his return he would have conducted the usual summer courses in his house, the two month intensive course which all of us have attended for several years during our training period. One of the young students whom he had taught till a few hours before his death, kept on asking loudly while sobbing incessantly, 'who will correct now whatever I have just learnt?' I suddenly realized how lucky we had been in having him teach us directly all these years and how privileged we had been in sharing so much time with him! Will we be able to inspire at least one disciple the way he had inspired so many of us?

Since the disciples from Mumbai, Delhi and Calcutta could arrive only the next day, in order to allow them to have his last *darshan*, his cremation had to be postponed for a day. When I returned the next day, the scene had changed considerably; his body was by then flanked by two thick walls of flowers and spontaneous songs and *bhajans* were being rendered by the local musicians, some of them composed specifically for him. Many of us embraced or held each others hands; we didn't need to speak much. The same sense of bewilderment was in each of us. At about two in the afternoon a bier made of bamboo and rope was brought to the courtyard to carry the body towards its final destination. There was commotion when the body was brought out and laid on it; the soles of Guruji's feet had been painted with *alta*, an impression taken of it on a white sheet of paper. While the body was placed on the ground for a final *darshan* I kept looking at it unable to move or think. I looked into the eyes of other people there; and found the same emptiness. The students from Mumbai and Delhi reached around that time; again tears, lamentation and scenes of desperation. I knew what they were going through and I felt privileged to have been able to hold his hand for more than an hour the previous day!

Then everything happened fast; a formal gun salute was given by the State Guards standing on both sides of the main gate and amidst shouts of *Ram Nam Sathya Hai* and shower of coloured powder thrown in the air, the body was placed in a black car and taken towards Puri. On the way was a brief halt at Raghurajpur, Guruji's native village, where his house is no more but where the temple built by him for his dear goddess Bhuasuni stands at the very entrance under a large banyan tree. He had been offered to her once when as a small child he fell ill with chickenpox and she had cured him at that time. This time she had wanted him all for herself. Raghurajpur is only 10 km away from Puri, the abode of Lord Jagannath. When I arrived at the *swarga dwara*, a small piece of land on the side of the sea, the fire had already started consuming the body. I have been told that in a spontaneous gesture all the dancers performed a group dance on the side of the pyre before it was lit. The flames were carried by the wind towards the sea; all the five elements were assembled in this place to receive back what was being slowly transformed into one of them. The transformation and evolution of the five elements from one to another was one of the favourite topics of Guruji who would each time give a slightly different version to his very personal theory of the evolution of the universe. I am sure this time also he would have talked about it!

Slowly the crowd started thinning; it was like after a performance, when the audience has dispersed, the lights of the stage are turned off and the artist comes out from the green room and finds himself alone in the night. I decided to stay till the end; there were only a few of us to watch the last small bones taken out from the flames and kept in a small clay pot sealed with mud. Guruji's younger brother, Bansidhar, who resembles him so much, received the pot in his hands and walked away without looking back. What is there in any case to look back for? Only dust remained which would soon be carried away by the wind. But even though his body is no more, his soul remains alive in each one of us.

APPENDIX 2

MILESTONES OF GURUJI'S LIFE

1924 Born in village Raghurajpur, district Puri, Orissa, to Chintamani Mohapatra, a *chitrakara* (traditional painter), and Siri Nani (1926 in official documents).

1929 He joins the *akhada* of Guru Balabhadra Sahu and continues training on *gotipua* dance for three years.

1932 He joins the Ras Leela troupe of Guru Mohansundar Dev Goswami in Puri and gradually becomes his most trusted disciple.

1941 Kelucharan's father passes away.

1943 He leaves the Ras Leela Party and works for about one year in the *pan* fields near Chandanpur for about 20-25 *paisa* a day. He also works for a month in Cuttack singing *sankirtan* for Banamali Sahu, a zamindar suffering from leprosy.

1944 He joins in Cuttack the Orissa Theatres founded by Kalicharan Pattanayak and remains there for a little less than one year at a salary of Rs. 7 per month.

1945 He joins as a director of the Radhakant Ras Party at Puri with a salary of Rs. 300 per month and stages *nataka Meerabai* his maiden directorial debut.

1946 He joins the newly formed Annapurna B Group in Cuttack at a salary of Rs. 15 per month and makes his maiden debut as a dancer in the role of Mahadev in the *nataka Devi*.

1947 He dances for the first time the item *Dashavatara*

in duet with female dancer Laxmipriya for the *nataka Sadhava Jhia*. The dance sequence is directed by Pankaj Charan Das.

1948 Guru Mohansundar Dev Goswami passes away. Kelucharan choreographs his first dance number for the *nataka Aloka* to be danced by Laxmipriya. The dance is in a mixed style of Manipuri, Odissi and Kathak and it is composed according to the teachings of Dayal Sharana.
Kelucharan marries Laxmipriya and both leave the Annapurna B Group.

1949 The couple, after a brief stint with the Annapurna A Group, settle down at Cuttack. Kelucharan composes dances for the Rupashree and Janata theatres where Laxmipriya is much in demand as actress and dancer.

1950 By now he has started to teach dance to few female dancers not associated with theatre. First students are: Sanjukta, Minati, Sadhana, Meera and Jayanti.

1952 Babulal Joshi starts the Kala Vikash Kendra (KVK) at Cuttack. First teacher is Mayadhar Rout who shares a room with Kelucharan and his family.

1953 Kelucharan joins as teacher at the KVK. With him most of his private students also join the Kendra. He teaches on a regular basis up to 1965. His salary starts from Rs. 20 and along the years increases up to Rs. 250 per month. Sanjukta performs first Odissi programme outside the state during the third annual function of the Children's Little Theatre at Calcutta.

1955 *Sakhi Gopala*, the first dance-drama entirely composed in Odissi style is choreographed jointly by Kelucharan and Pankaj Babu and presented at Delhi for the Industrial Fair.

1956 Kelucharan presents the recital of Priyambada for the 3rd Inter University Youth Festival in Delhi in which she wins the first prize.

1957 Jayantika is formed at Cuttack by a group of scholars and gurus including Dev Prasad Das, Pankaj Babu and Kelucharan for the purpose of systematizing the Odissi dance form.

1958 In January Kelucharan presents Sanjukta's dance during the All India Dance Seminar at Madras as part of the 31st Conference of the Music Academy.

In April he accompanies Jayanti's dance at the All India Dance Seminar organized by Sangeet Natak Akademi at New Delhi. On both the occasions Kalicharan Pattanaik reads a paper on Odissi.

1959 Kelucharan contracts tuberculosis. He has to abstain from work for about 6 months. In the meantime the meetings of Jayantika slowly dwindle to an end.

1961 Kelucharan accompanies Priyambada's dance at Sapru House in New Delhi. On this occasion she dances eleven pieces, all presented in separate sequences.

He buys a piece of land in Cuttack for Rs. 1,500 and over a period of four years, builds his house.

1964 Kelucharan gets sick with high fever after over-exerting himself for the rehearsals of *Krishna Leela* to be presented at Bombay by KVK.

1965 Ratikanta, Kelucharan's son, is born. The entire family shifts to the newly constructed house at Samanta Sahi.

1966 Kelucharan gets the Sangeet Natak Akademi award for Odissi dance.

1967 He participates in the Seminar on *Gita Govinda* in Delhi jointly organized by Sangeet Natak Akademi and Lalit Kala Akademi with two new *ashtapadi* danced by Kumkum Das. On special request he gives a presentation on the next day, this being his first presentation of *Gita Govinda* outside the state.

He accompanies Sanjukta as part of an Indian dance delegation to Russia in his first trip to a foreign country.

1968 He accompanies Sonal Mansingh in a series of eight shows in Madras; the first one, at the Museum Theatre, is attended by Rukmini Devi.

He starts conducting summer courses at KVK which are attended by local as well as outside students.

He starts teaching for few months at a stretch at the Nritya Niketan, a school started by Hare Krishna Behera at Delhi.

1968 Kelucharan and Sonal are invited to perform at Kala Kshetra in Madras.

1974 He teaches for a few months at Triveni Kala Sangam in New Delhi.

He receives the Padmashri award.
He choreographs the Hindi version of the *Gita Govinda* with music by Pandit Jasraj in Bombay.

1975 He comes back to the stage by playing the role of Bishu Maharana in the ballet *Konarka* staged at Cuttack.

1979 He starts conducting short courses of one month duration at the Gandharva Mahavidyalaya in New Delhi. He performs on stage the *ashtapadi Priye Charusheele*; this marks the re-emergence of Kelucharan as performer. In the next two decades memorable performances on stage were to follow.

1980 He starts conducting short courses of one month duration at Padatik Dance Centre in Calcutta.

1981 He starts conducting short courses of one month duration at National Centre for Performing Arts at Bombay.
He dances for the first time two *ashtapadis* in duet with Kumkum Das during a performance at Benaras.

1982 He participates in the first Festival of India held in London with Sanjukta.

1983 He joins Odissi Research Centre at Bhubaneswar, headed by Kumkum Mohanty for an initial honorarium of Rs. 4,000 per month. He is attached to the Centre up to 1994.

1987 He is conferred with the Kalidasa award by the Madhya Pradesh Government.
He shifts from his Cuttack residence to government accommodation in Bhubaneswar.

1988 He gets the Padma Bhushan award from Government of India.

1989 He suffers his first mild heart attack and is admitted to the intensive care unit of the main hospital in Bhubaneswar.

1990 He undergoes a triple by-pass surgery at Birla Heart Centre in Calcutta. A film on him *Bhavantarana* is made by Kumar Shahani.

1994 He founds his own institution, Srjan and shifts to his own house in Bhimatangi, Bhubaneswar.

1995 He receives the title of 'Officer of the Order of Art and Culture' from the French Ministry of Culture.

1996 He receives Dr B.C. Roy National Award instituted by the Medical Council of India.

2000 He receives the Padma Vibhushan award from Government of India.

2001 He terminates the construction of a small temple for goddess Bhuasuni in his native village Raghurajpur and perfoms the inaguration rituals.

2002 He receives the Gupta Award from the Gupta Foundation of Elluru.

2003 He receives the *Commendeur dans l'Ordre des Arts et Des Letters* from the Ministry of Culture, Government of France.

2004 He passes away on 7 April, due to massive heart attack.

APPENDIX 3

DANCE COMPOSITIONS BY GURUJI

DANCE-DRAMAS

1953 *Kishori Kanhu*
1954 *Urvashi*
1955 *Amrit Manthana*, *Anadi Sangeeta*, *Ras Leela*, *Sakhi Gopala*
1956 *Palli Gatha*, *Chitrangada*
1957 *Jibanara Chhanda*, *Pancha Puspa*, *Nada Nupura*, *Madhana Bhasma*, *Jeevan Darshana*
1958 *Krishna Gatha*, *Pujarini*, *Mahanadi*, *Chandrika*, *Konarka Jagarana*
1959 *Meghadoot*, *Kumara Sambhava*, *Sapan Nayaka*
1960 *Pancha Purnami*
1961 *Braja Leela*, *Sri Jagannatha*, *Ramayana*, *Gita Govinda*, *Bhagavat Gita*
1962 *Amara Bharati*, *Tapaswini*, *Chandrabhaga*, *Buddhadeva*
1963 *Vikrama Urvashi*, *Shakuntala*, *Bharat Mata*
1964 *Bhanu Sinhara Padavali*, *Krishna Leela*, *Ambrapalli*
1965 *Mahabharata*
1970 *Kanchi Vijay*
1975 *Geet Govinda* (Hindi)
1981 *Ramcharitamanasa*
1983 *Champu*
1989 *Chandrabhaga*

1990 *Vastra Harana*, *Kanchi Abhijan*
1991 *Dasanana*
1992 *Ekalavya*
1994 *Dushyanta Shakuntala*, *Utkala mauda mani*, *Yagnyaseni*
1995 *Chand Ashoka*
1996 *Kurukshetra*
1998 *Sudama Daridra Bhanjana*, *Mathamani pradana*, *Balya Leela*
2000 *Rutu Samhara*
2002 *Krishna Sudama*

PALLAVI

1957 Basanta
1959 Kalyani
1965 Mohana, Shankara Bharana
1966 Saveri
1971 Gatibheda
1972 Arabhi
1979 Hamsadhwani, Khamaj
1981 Bihag, Kirwani
1983 Belahari
1993 Mukhari
1996 Singhendra

ASHTAPADI

1958 *Lalita labanga lata*
1961 *Yami he kamiha sharanam*, *Yahi Madhava*
1962 *Pashyati dishi dishi*
1963 *Hariiha Magdha*
1967 *Kuru yadunandana*, *Dhira samire*, *Sakhi he*
1968 *Rase harimiha*
1972 *Mugdhe madhu mathanam*
1974 *Mamiyam chalita vilokya*
1977 *Kapi madhuripuna*
1983 *Radha vadana*
1984 *Srita kamala kucha mandala*
1988 *Madhave ma Kuru*
1993 *Kisalaya sayana tale*
1995 *Samudita vadane*, *Ramate Yamuna*

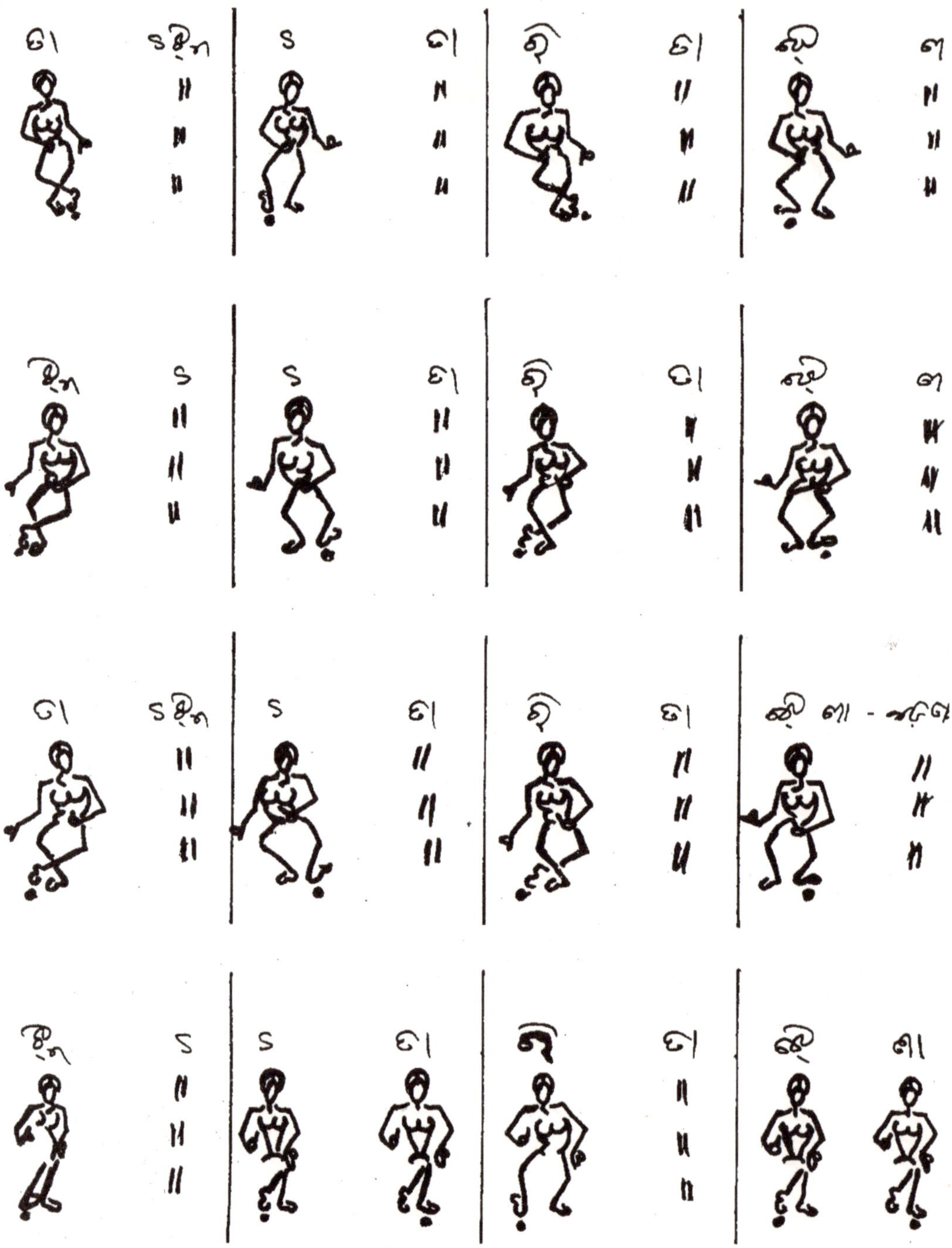